Tell Tale Pug Tail & Everything Else

POOJA
PASRICHA

INDIA • SINGAPORE • MALAYSIA

ISBN 979-8-89186-394-1

Breathe.

Dream and write.

It's the only way,

I know how to cleanse.

For most of us love isn't easy or simple.

Nuts showed us it really is.

Dedicated to my 'Light of Love'.

FOREWORD

Death is like a burglar that sneaks in and simply takes away what you hold dear without a warning.

We also remain delusional about mortality.

We as a family were completely unprepared and had no clue as to where Nuts could have a final resting place when Death decided to steal him.

The situation worsened because we were devastated and heart broken. Thinking sanely was hard. So as if in a trance, we drove around in our car looking and delaying, denying reality. He lay lifeless in my lap wrapped in his blanket. The longer I held him, the more intense the illogical desire for a miracle became.

We eventually chose a spot nestled between two trees close to our flat and laid him to rest. We also installed an iron bench in his memory.

It has served as a resting place for all who pass by and in the bargain ensured that Nuts will always have the company he so loved.

I wrote 'The Blue Bench' as a depiction of his resting place.

Whilst he was alive, I'd tell him I'd plant Chrysanthemums over his grave. I did not keep my word.

The flower thus holds centre stage on the cover of this book.

Most of my writing has been inspired by my 'Zoon' as I liked to address him.

Illogical and fantastic as it may sound, a part of me hopes Nuts is aware of this ode to him.

I am grateful to you, dear reader, for choosing to be a part of my writing journey.

Hope the collection or parts of it resonate with your finer senses.

CONTENTS

CYNOPHILE

- The God Delusion 13
- Me And Him 18
- Nuts And The Humans 21
- The Moon Me And Him 24
- Dogs Always 26
- Faith 31
- Rarely, When Nuts Was Human 32
- Odour 33
- How We Named The Cat 35
- How Dogs Love 36
- The Blue Bench 39

ODE TO GAIA

- Liberation 43
- The Dirge 45
- Alive 49

EVERYTHING ELSE

- Butterfly Effect 53
- True 56
- Comfort 57
- The Final Will 58

- Privileged 59
- Happy Meal 61
- Abandon 62
- Peony 63
- Umbilical Cord 65
- Peace 66
- Glow 69
- Love Story 70
- Time 72
- Dear God 75
- Doll 76
- Coffee 77
- Joy 78
- The Believer 81
- Irony 83
- How To Love Right 85
- Say Something 87
- Promises 88
- What's Love Got To Do With It 89
- Blame It On The Name 92
- How To Live After You Die 95
- Mirror! Mirror! 97
- Nritya 98
- Hope 100
- Home 103
- On Kashmir 107

- Memory Bank 111
- Letters 114
- God, Please Show Yourself 118
- Worlds Apart 121

RIB TICKLERS

- Ptv (Pre-Teen Teen Virus) 125
- The 'Mother' Tongue 129
- On Vanity 132
- The Book Thief 138
- Quite A Spectacle - I 140
- Quite A Spectacle - II 144
- Quite A Spectacle - III 145
- M.O.M. 149
- Books 153
- Just A Mom 154
- The Inheritance 161
- Family Matters 166
- OCD 172

XX CHROMOSOME

- Fear Is Not The Key 179
- The X Factor 184
- The Heart Wants What It Wants 187
- Esse 191

THE X Y Z GENERATION

- What Children Want 197
- Dear Know-It-All 200

THE FLAUTIST

- Ode To Krishna 205
- Kanha 209
- The Favourite 212

Acknowledgements 217

Addendum 219

• • •

CYNOPHILE

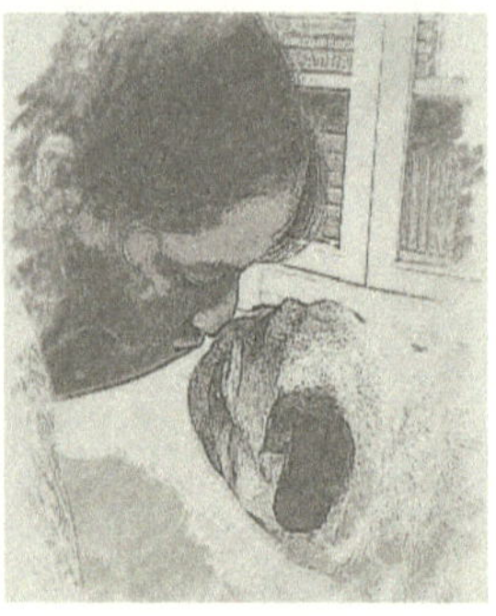

When you decide to make a dog a part of your life, you will be blessed with a lifetime of unconditional love.

THE GOD DELUSION

At some point in time,
most married couples,
decide to play God.

The urge to procreate,
truly surpasses sanity.
It may be a momentary lapse of reason,
but ends up as a lifetime of prison!

To willingly, want your life usurped,
and your anatomy completely warped.
Clearly, you are totally deluded.

Get a pet I say,
and you won't regret it a day.
If you want to love and be loved.

The one you hope to make,
in your image,
will poop and pee,
bawl and howl,
demand to be fed, cleaned and clothed.
And,
it's an illusion,

if you think it ends at some point here.
Not a chance.
Nada!
It's Hotel California.

You,
turn into a slave.
And,
will willingly serve,
this little 12-inch mistress/master,
till it's perhaps 6ft or further.

The gurgling and angelic smile stage,
I admit, is quite intoxicating.
But it's just a mirage.

You wish you did not really coax them,
to start using syllables,
or forming words.
Sooner than later,
it's near impossible,
to match up to their not so traditional
choice of expression.
Facial or verbal.
So, it's okay, if your kid just gurgles away!!

What of the inconceivable joy,
when your little girl or boy,
stumbles and staggers to a maiden step.
Serious error of judgement!
Because, where these feet begin to travel,
will be a mystery to unravel.
So, if your bonny baby,
wants to sit on his bum,
just let him!!

So, you coochie coo,
and smother your princess,
with kisses,
and happily clad her,
in short skirts and halters,
and frilly bloomers under.
You should have really used a veil.
Because for your daughter,
the real fashion,
icon,
will be the emperor with nearly no clothes.

All notions, definitions,
of romantic alliances,
with your spouse,
are greatly altered.
All that you end up desiring is to nestle in the inviting folds
of your bed.

There are many occasions,
when you are allowed,
but a mere inch of space in your own bed,
because the little thing you made,
barged into your room,
because 'something' barged into his.
The little thing lays splayed,
generously between you and your spouse,
with its little hands all over your face,
or even inside your nostril or mouth.

Of course,
when this same little being, at 3 feet,
becomes a bigger being,
and attains greater height,
this being then,
has a password protected,
multi-layered security system,
in place,
if you need to access his/her space.
And,
have no doubts.
Trespassers WILL be prosecuted.

So, I say get a pet.
Leave playing God
to God!!

As for me,

I do have two to spare.

No charge.

You can have them.

At a NO RETURN policy.

Because me and my spouse are getting a pet.

ME AND HIM

The warmest place is inside a hug.

I have to leave.

He knows that.

He simply refuses to eat.

(By the way, what his highness has been served is a treat he normally cannot resist,

and has exhibited abominable etiquette in the past).

He sulks in a corner, sitting hunched.

Mouth sagging, pouting, almost like a child.

He'd cry,

If he could.

Well, I cajole,
play a tyrant's role.
I beg and I plead,
tempt and lure.

But he is steadfast.
Stubborn and hurt.
Reticent.
Blackmailing, blackguard bum,
throwing a silent tantrum.

I hug him warmly.
Coo in his ears lovingly.
Nope!
I am at the end of the rope.
I am getting edgy,
frustrated and angry.

I then entice him with a little walk.
Aha! A trifle sparkle.
His eyes blink,
a little wavering,
a little giving in, bending.
Encouraged, I head towards the door.
Nah! He decides, slumps back to his corner.
What an awful bother!!

So, what's a girl to do?
I give up this once,
Do I really have a choice?

Some other time Mr Cruise.
My conversation, (on my cell) is brief and terse.
My friend only sighs.
I am known to be capricious.
They know, He holds all the cards.

I do believe,
as I spot his face,
from the corner of my eye,
that he has donned a smug smile,
and slyly moved his seat next to mine!!

The masterful eavesdropper.
The artful conspirator,
is suddenly ravenous!!!
And before I can even slip out of my pumps,
he's let out a series of boorish burps.

Nudges me - Thank you!
Me - You're welcome, you troll.
Him - Shall we?
Me - Yeah, let's go dude.

Legs in dance mode,
We're off for our evening stroll.

NUTS AND THE HUMANS

He was the most benign and harmless being I have encountered. Unassuming and even tempered, his patience was worth emulating.

The cat we owned for a short while, used him for target practice, pouncing at him from all angles, at any and every opportunity.

All the while Nuts maintained a stoic stance, like an old grandpop humouring a hyperactive grandchild.

So, it was rather amusing to witness reactions of fear from people when they crossed paths with him, at home or elsewhere especially in the lift, the most social space in our apartment building!!

True to his inherent trait, he believed everyone loved everyone and was equally gleeful to interact as he was. Unfortunately, reciprocal enthusiasm seldom came his way.

We encountered all kinds of people with varied frames. Some would emulate the avian family and flap their arms wildly squawking quite like birds in distress and scoot to a corner in the lift. Others would become statue like, as if playing dead when facing a predator in the wild. Each time someone reacted adversely at his sight or avoided him, Nuts looked completely perplexed and he would don the softest expression and wag his curly tail in an attempt to ease the humans. This too would be met with squirming.

There were parents taking their responsibilities of keeping their offspring safe, very seriously. They'd hide their children behind their ample behinds protecting them from this 'monster'. 'Monster' continued to look lovingly at kids. He simply adored them.

Unbeknownst to these parents I had sneaked a few decent friendships between the kids and him.

It was a well-kept secret and the children played their parts well.

Some merely took a look at who was going to be taking a ride with them down to the basement and abandoned the idea of taking the lift altogether.

A few would scream as though someone stabbed them and run at the very sight of him.

A certain friend screeched like a banshee and threatened to climb all over my newly acquired beige sofas if I didn't get our little man out of her way.

Ironically, there is no antidote for the human bite.

Of course, there were those aggressive ones who were very vocal about the rights of lift usage claiming human exclusivity. In such cases, I'd glare angrily while Nutsy Boy would make a move towards camaraderie.

If I had my way, I'd have had my favourite being do a growl for a growl.

But he was not human. He was humane and kind and love was the only language he knew.

I, on the other hand, am human and hence continued to do the growling for him.

THE MOON ME AND HIM

The moon, resplendent, joyous and glorious,
shone softly.
Benign and generous,
bestowing peace.

We sat by the brook,
in quiet harmony,
letting the calm serenity engulf us.
The moon beams, cascading playfully across the water.
Weaving dreams and carrying wishes.
Shimmering, dancing and glittering.

A cobbled pathway forming underwater,
with the glinting pebbles,
enticing us along.
A misty spray,
Exchanging all our woes for joy.

This was our forever place.

The deep blue blanket,
studded with diamonds,
was a mirage of impossible longings.
The medley of the cicadas and the dancing

glow worms,
enthralled us with their magical performance.
Infused with intoxicating odours,
the soft breeze,
enslaved us.

Inebriated,
we sat side by side.
He nuzzled close,
his cold nose brushing against my hand,
and placed his head on my knee.

We,
our souls as one,
bathed in the languid moonlight,
that washed our hearts with pleasure.

We sat, with nothing but the truth,
of life and love,
with only the language of nature between us.

DOGS ALWAYS

Husband, kids and dog in that order.
Had it been the other way around earlier,
that would have been IT.
DOG.
Oh! without a doubt, dog.
I'd go ONLY for the dog.

I usually like to start my day in the morning.
Yes! it's true, morning is my thing.
Of course, the only other sane creature who likes it, is the dog.

We both simply adore the morning stroll,
the sound of silence,
the fresh breeze,
watching the not yet extinct and on the verge of extinction species of birds, in various modes of activities.
And meeting fellow creatures. (Only dogs here, I usually ignore the owners, it's mutual really,
I am a privileged human).

Meanwhile,
found in various stages of deep slumber, are:

Husband with a smile, always with a smile.
Serenity etched across his unblemished features.
The only blessed guy with the world's most beautiful dreams.
God's favourite man.

He usually wakes up still in his dreamlike stupor,
which is rudely shattered by my crass crow like squawking,
when I cannot stand that smile any longer.

There's a song for him,
My God! the songwriter, he was a seer!!
It's written for him.
It's an ode to him.
Resonating perfectly.
"Watching the wheels go round and round....."

Children, both having had a lot of trouble putting eyelids over eyes through the night.
The magical, unreal, real, virtual reality, unreality having kept them enrapt and entrapped.
A little slacking by way of sleep,
would be social hara-kiri!
Blasphemy to miss updates.
The next episode of others' lives.
Bare it all self-portraits, the complications of love lives.
And all the 'competitive' fun everyone has.

It's a kind of social omerta.

Code of voyeurism!!

Perhaps when the morning rays must have begun stinging the eyes,

they must have shut involuntarily.

Sleep is such a party pooper!

To get them to function like humans and not owls,

I do my bit of slamming doors and I mess with the rooms' fuse boxes.

This one is a winner all the way, especially,

during the hot summer months.

So, this pair awakens,

somewhere around lunch,

only to munch.

And I must add, the husband and kids come from the lineage of the Arab Sultanate.

Or perhaps, they are reincarnated Pharaohs.

I, on the other hand, got born a slave.

Unlike my favourite being(dog),

they don't feel guilty about the mess they make.

Royalty always has a cleaning entourage.

That would naturally be me!

The dog exudes so much love, warmth and gratefulness.

Above all its my company that he really likes.

We can hang out together all day without him feeling stifled or bored.

He never sulks, when scolded.

The scenario is quite something else.

when it involves the husband and kids.

One becomes a martyr.

the other two, a nightmare.

Children exhibit something close to love only when they run out of moolah or are hungry.

I am usually accused of not giving them space and being too nosey.

I admit I actually am.

Juicy teen gossip,

is more entertaining than any melodrama.

I manage to extract quite a dose from the kids.

Later, they do regret telling me.

The husband remains in his nirvana state, bliss and comfort at all levels.

Tea, coffee and dreams.

The dog knows when I have to go out.

Quietly, he segues to his 'sadness' spot,

remaining there till after I return and then I am welcomed back with a bouncing gait and a wagging tail.

As for the offsprings in their respective dens,

wish that I rather took on a mountaineering expedition, lasting 12 months a year.

That would be something to cheer for!!!

Meanwhile, John Lennon continues to inspire the man of the house.

Silent, tacit communication,

I have with all three.

Dog and me, "love, love and more love..."

Kids and me, "leave, leave, leave...."

Husband and me, "I wish I was single again.!!!"

FAITH

Human sighing witnessing nature's beauty.

Lola (local lady doggo)**:** Hey! Never seen God before?

Human: Huh!! What?!! Obviously not!

Lola: Strange! Because I bask in His love every day!

RARELY, WHEN NUTS WAS HUMAN

He was sitting, all by himself, moping. He seemed to have the blues.

So, I did what I thought would help ease his woes.

I went up to him and tried to kiss and hug him.

He didn't want any of it.

Told me to be gone with my silly love.

He'd deal with his problems on his own.

Think my kids rubbed off on him too much!!

ODOUR

It was simple with him because it was our hearts that talked. Words fumbled and sounded gibberish.

Nuts had his spot. The sadness spot. If he were a turtle he'd have simply gotten in his shell. Since he was a dog he needed to find these niches to be sad.

Even his sadness was simple.

He wanted a full house. That is when he'd settle his bum against a wall or cosy up in his bed and sleep like a log. Face twitching and legs making a running motion. He'd yip like a pup at times. His snoring could rattle a dead man to life!

Take one family member out of the equation, he'd go into his blue mood and sleep erratically with a constant eye at the main door.

He'd rather we never went to work or anywhere else!!

As for me, I don't have any safe spot to get by the blues. The causes of my sadness are far more complex and not easily overcome.

I have tried washing them away in the shower hoping to see them flow down the drain. It doesn't really work.

Sadness, perhaps has a distinct odour. It must smell dank and mouldy. Musty.

I think he would smell it off me because he'd sit next to me and rest his chin on my knee.

We'd sit so, till my nerves began to soothe and I was warm with his love. Till a calm settled over me.

Calm also must have an odour. Like vanilla essence maybe.

He'd smell that too because he would start nudging me towards the kitchen.

HOW WE NAMED THE CAT

Cat: Hey Gramps! Can I play with your tail?

Nuts grunts, turns the other way.

Cat bounces, swipes at the dog's tail anyway.

Nuts and I exchange a mutual look of exasperation.

Cat goes ballistic leaping all over Nuts.

Nuts: What a Doofus!

Me: That's a good name for this retard.

Meanwhile, newly baptised cat, being royally ignored, tries new tactics.

Doofus: C'mon old man, at least let me cuddle with you.

Nuts: Bah! Whatever!

HOW DOGS LOVE

There is no better teacher than dogs if we want to learn to love.

Simply as if there really is nothing more to it.

And truly there really isn't.

We know that too.

But it's still difficult for us to love simply.

So often, I was hurried in my dealings with Nuts. I just wanted to get it all over with.

His walks, his meal and he always complied easily with my brusqueness.

He understood my inherent human-ness.

Sometimes I was moody and upset. He would then, just sit next to me, his head on my knee. He'd tell me he was there for me always.

He missed family members when they were away. His ears drooped and his eyes would become sad.

Sometimes he'd just put his nose against you and take deep whiffs, as if trying to embed the memory of you in himself, so as to never forget you.

We on the other hand, have short and selective memories for people and acts of kindness.

We carry baggage of the saddest kind.

We house guilt that affects all our relationships. We harbour resentment against our own, not strangers whom we encounter unpleasantly sometimes. Strangers don't matter. It is easy to be kind to them. It is easy to forgive and forget. Because they are not the ones who break your heart irreparably.

We deceive our own.

There were times when we had to leave Nuts home for our chores or our entertainment. We had the best welcome when we returned. A bouncing gait and a crazily wagging tail asking how our day was and how happy he was to see us.

No-one loved like him.

He had a sweet tooth but being his caretakers, we got to decide what was good for him and what wasn't. He was satisfied with just a wee lick. He believed we knew best.

You can't deprive a human of something they love or desire, edible or otherwise and have them believe in you. Or love you unconditionally.

Without a shred of doubt, I know, the heightened sense of smell that dogs possess is not limited to only edibles. Nuts could smell emotions and displayed understanding beyond human capabilities.

He comprehended our words, was sensitive to our feelings, adapted to us, accepted us in our various flawed aspects.

For us humans, love is deeply complicated and never enough.

Technically, being of the same species, we speak the same language but ever so often we cannot understand the other.

THE BLUE BENCH

I sit with Nuts.

I sit and I listen.

I listen,

to the trees whisper,

the birds trill and tweet, chirp and caw,

engrossed in their cacophonous fracas.

I watch their antics as they hop from branch to branch,
careening and fluttering between leaves.

Carefree, full of life's joys.

I smell the fragrance of all the blossoms with the passing breeze.

The chirruping squirrels making a racket, scooting about.
Their bushy tails sending out signals of various kinds.
Oh, they have a full schedule!
No room for boredom!!

I sit with Nuts.
I listen.
To him.
I tell him about me.
I tell him a million times how much I miss him.
He listens.
Patiently, full of love as always.
I sit there to swallow his love.

I sit there to remember.
I sit there seeking forgiveness.

I inhale peace.

•••

ODE TO GAIA

The True Altruist

When she shares her bounties, you almost, almost feel all is right with the world.

LIBERATION

The day she found herself,
she wore her beauty inside out.

Trapped sunlight beneath her eyelids,
and glowing embers lined her eyes with kohl.

Allowed the breeze to do her hair,
to wrap itself around her.
It gave her wings.
And she soared light as air.

Infused her being with the fragrance of the flowers,
and butterflies sat on her eyelashes.
Bees whispered sweet nothings in her ears.
Butterflies kissed her cheeks.

She clasped her dreams in tight fists,
and only opened her palms wide to the teal skies.
Like dandelions, they soared and wafted, unfettered.
Then, they burst into a million stars.

She, borrowed some freedom from the birds,
laughter from the rivers,
resilience from the trees,
learnt the language of the leaves.

Light as a feather, she floated.
Dressed in love,
breathing in happiness.
She segued into the arms of the nurturer.

Her home became lost in a house.
In a melee of retrogressive technology.

THE DIRGE

The sensation of caressing the deep blue skies,
fills her with immense pleasure.
She can almost feel the wind.
Buoyant and gay,
playful, teasing her.
Gentle at times,
like the soft lapping waves of the sea,
and wild, turbulent,
at others.

She reminisces.

Bouncing along the balls of cotton,
luring her.
Sometimes as a rabbit,
or a graceful mare.
Menacing at times,
growling and baring their dark side.

She yearns for the crisp fresh air,
the rain-washed countryside,
the moist grass,
and the newly bathed trees,
their leaves glistening in the mild golden hue.

She remembers beauty,
in the pearls she splatters from her drenched body.
In a single beam,
housing a magical display of colours.
In the magnificent arc with no beginning or end.

She remembers,
reaching for the elixir in this kaleidoscopic enigma.

Her palate still tingles,
with the delectable ambrosia,
aching for the generous array of blossoms.

She remembers,
sliding down moonbeams,
and swallowing dew drops.

Her eyes closed,
she sings.
With the vision of freedom.

That is something they cannot take from her.

Like a Prima Donna,
her aria at a crescendo.
Her heart weeps.
Her voice carries all these memories.
She needs them.

Trapped in her golden boudoir,
her once vibrant plume,
is faded and dull.
Her pride,
clipped and shorn,
lies limp, futile and worn.

It's a mournful dirge,
A trill of longing and sadness.

She sings to her love.
She sings in defiance.

Her song is her elegy.

This could be my song.
She could be me.

ALIVE

As I walked along the lavish, indulgent meadows,
a quiet serenity washed over me.

Inebriated and hedonistic with pleasure,
somnolent and languid with the calm,
my eyelids heavy with sleep.
Enveloped in a heavenly trance,
I lay in the soft welcoming grass.
With, the vast azure extending beyond now and forever.
Enfolding me in its generous embrace.

I felt I was special.
Elite.
An honoured audience.
Nature revealing itself with complete abandon.
Basking in all its attention,
and witnessing magic.
I set my soul free.

Wandering,
I became the breeze blowing across meadows,
gliding softly, lazily.
I eased between trees,
hearing them whisper beautiful secrets.
I was a flock of wild chattering and chirping birds,
composing cheerful melodies.

I melted into streams and rivers,
sharing their gurgling laughter and happy songs.

I danced and swayed with the joyous daffodils.
I smelt the earth.
Wisdom of an eon washing over me.

Reliving the memories of a lifetime.
I transformed into lush pastures,
tasting dew drops on my lips.

I was everywhere.
My senses acute and insatiable.
This is the only way I knew how to be alive.

My mortal being in its human form,
a mere speck, inconsequential.
Seeking refuge,
seeking solace
In nature.

• • •

EVERYTHING ELSE

There is a vault of stories waiting to be told;
The trees might just whisper a secret;
the wind, unravel tales from around the world;
the clouds may rumble with laughter;
One only has to listen.

A kindness from a stranger;
A warm embrace;
A wagging tail;
One only needs to acknowledge all the love;

For all who yearn for a taste of life;
A potpourri of everything.

BUTTERFLY EFFECT

The illness had been long, too long.
She has been on the brink, on the edge,
there was hopeless resignation, despair.
She'd barely clung to life.

But then, the stars aligned in her favour.
Blessed with the miracle of life, she rose.
Unsure, trembling, wobbly.
Instinctively, she was drawn to those born of her heart.

Ruffled her son's curly mop,
whispered sweet nothings in her daughter's ears.
Kissed them a million times.
How she had longed for her children.
Nuzzling, she wanted to breathe them in, infuse them within her.
As their smiles lit up the house,
she was born anew.

After months of anguish and an inconsequential existence,
she wanted to fly, to be known, to make a difference.
She wanted to paint the world in the colours of love.

The sun kissed her lashes,
the breeze wafted through her hair.
She smelt jasmine, she smelt roses.
The azure seemed to lap like waves in a deep blue ocean.
She inhaled deeply, greedily,
all of the fresh morning air, filling her insides with life,
let the sun linger over her face.
She closed her eyes, awash with gratitude.

She smiled warmly at a man standing by the curb.
She reminded him of the love of his life.
Suddenly, the wait held no meaning,
impulsively, he hailed a cab.

She snuggled the runt of a litter, love flowing from her to him.
A young girl out for a morning run saw this bundle of fur.
He was just what she wanted.
Love found him a home.

She thanked the local sweepers.
They smiled back and a friendship started.

An old woman at the park,
clutching her mobile,
a nervous melancholy surrounding her.
She pines for one made of her own flesh and blood.

Abandoned for years over an inconsequential difference.

Tears of loneliness run like rivulets, her damp wrinkles crusted with salt.

Oblivious of her magic, she sat by the old woman,

clasping her hand firmly, letting the woman grieve.

When her phone, old and outdated just like her, rang, she simply stared at the screen!

Unsure of both her sight and hearing!

It was a ringtone she hadn't changed in years.

And as her magic, the magic of love and kindness unfolded, it filled many empty hearts and healed all the cracks on their souls.

Filling them with hope.

Addendum:

You must try this at home with your loved ones and even strangers!

Who knows a fine blessing may come your way!

TRUE

There is but one true you,
prominent and dominant,
when no one's watching you.
The world does not know *that* you.
But you do.
Can you live with it?

COMFORT

It's all in the comfort of being,
that beauty lies.
Steadfast and stolid like a tree.

It's in the stillness of being,
that peace is found.
Calming like the lapping waves of the ocean, softly kissing the shores.

It's in the glory of being,
that radiates joy.
Resplendent, glowing likes the sun,
warming hearts and the hearth in its embrace.

Loving yourself,
to being who you are.
There is no greater truth.

When you rejoice in yourself,
you will begin to live.

THE FINAL WILL

The absolute and irrefutable division of your materialistic, earthly belongings.

It's quite straightforward, uncomplicated.

I leave item 'x' to son, property 'y' to daughter and so on.

Naturally, you imagine the apportioned things would satisfy your progeny.

Bring out memories of you. Each object carrying a tale, an associated anecdote.

Maybe there'd be laughter, a flashback of their growing years. Perhaps a few tears would be shed reminiscent of unhappy moments.

It's satisfying to know that which was dear to you, would find a place, a designated spot in your babies' homes.

The thought of being somewhat alive even after you are physically gone is kind of reassuring.

It is the saddest aspect of being human, the desire to be immortal in some way.

The yearning to be remembered well.

However, what is truly challenging is leaving behind the legacy of love.

Will the children be satiated?

Will you be in their thoughts as having loved them well?

PRIVILEGED

No, I am not a prude.
It's just this,
what a terribly spoilt brood!!
Silver spoons,
and privileges.

Endowed with the Ovarian Lottery.
The lackadaisical procrastinators.
Childhood is passé.
Naiveté lost.
To be a sot, and fill your lungs with soot.
What kind of statement is that?

Staggering gait,
slurred speech,
misplaced time and dimension.
Misplaced notions of liberty and dignity.

Dignity,
Ensconced and wrapped like delicate silk,
in a warm sanctuary, for years.
By those whose eyes, are crinkled with crow's feet.
And the truth of their love etched across their features.
One wrinkle for every passing year.
Each streak of silver, witness to their faith.
In the ones that were born of them.

They don't know,
faith became sullied.

They remain delusional.

Sometimes,
it's just as well.

HAPPY MEAL

Families that eat together, stay together.

Perhaps.

But families that laugh together, last forever.

So, the next time you sit down to dine with Family, carry with you,

a jar full of laughter,

a pocketful of sunshine and

some craziness up your sleeve.

At the end,

each one will be truly satiated,

not just with food.

Of course, then, it can appropriately be called a 'Happy Meal!!'

A lot more special than the one at ***.

ABANDON

Within the confines of these walls,
lies my freedom.
Here is where I can be.
I fly, I dream.
I soar.
My limbs ache with pleasure.
I want more.

To lose myself in movement.
To drown myself in rhythm.

The world outside is Maya.
This, here, is my reality.

PEONY

A flower is the prettiest smile you'll ever see.
A nosegay of happiness.

The petals, unfurling all the cheer.
It must be the sense of contentment,
that makes it glow with so much joy.

It would be nice to be a flower.
To smile and dance to a breeze,
with the sun kissing my face,
and pearls of rain to adorn me.

To turn to silver with the shining moon.
To welcome the bees,
and hear whispers of butterfly wings.
The humming bird would serenade me.
And I would yield all my sweetness.

It would be nice to be a flower.
A tulip, a rose, a lily?
I think I'd be glad to be a Peony.

UMBILICAL CORD

I really have nothing to say.
But I call you, I message you.
Just to hear your voice.
To know you are well.

Love can be so inconsequential.
So routine.
So ordinary.

I walk around in your room.
Organising your cupboard, (which really is quite in order).
I stretch the ends of the bedcover.
Run my hands over it, dusting it.
Sometimes I sit and look at all your pictures.
Waves of nostalgia engulfing me.
Did I do alright?
Was I good enough?
Did I fill you up with love to last you a lifetime?

I look for signs.
Read between the lines, for some hidden meaning, an unresolved issue.

I cannot let go,
of
the life that I am responsible for.

PEACE

He embodied peace.
Within.

Crow's feet adorned his face.
The creases crinkled around his eyes like a bunch of smiles.

His soft brown eyes,
they were deep pools of kindness.
As if he would engulf your entire pain in those calm limpid orbs.

There was a reassurance of goodness about his demeanour. He inspired faith.

The warmth of his aura was like manna.
Like the sun's rays on one's skin on a cold winter day.

His deep baritone voice, almost reminded one of the lamas chanting Buddhist mantras.

Her skin, the colour of honey.
Flawless.
Ageless.
Perfectly sculpted.

She could be a sculptor's muse.
Danced like a swan.
Her limbs, fluid like water..

Her soul raw.

She needed to wear kind clothes, soft and gentle on her skin and heart.
To envelop her in warmth, an asylum for her body ravaged by harsh words.

Her skin could not bear the coarseness of cloth, it would scrape her soul.

Always clad in the finest satins, her scars felt cocooned and safe.

Her refuge lay in the folds of muted softness.

His words were like a gentle drizzle,
oozing slowly into her pores.
Washing her insides,
delicately and precisely.

Her body slumped with relief every time he spoke, his voice like soft whispers on her skin.
A balm to her battered soul.

The broad chest felt like home, with the calm beating of his heart, a regular dependable pulse.
A shield.

And just like that, one day, she began clothing herself in the hand spun weaves she so yearned to don.
The weaves felt like her second skin.

GLOW

There is no flaw in my love.
It's pure and true.
It's absolute.

It is you who is like a sieve.
It is you who has a void.
You can't seem to hold the love in.

But you shine.
Because of my love.

And your insides are soothed.
As I touch each part of you and love flows through you.

And, as it leaves through your pores, your body glows.

I will continue to love you.
till all the cracks are healed.

Till you glow on the inside.

LOVE STORY

He rummages frantically through his brain for lost memories, as if looking through his old coat pocket for a letter he was sure he had kept, for the love of his life.

Like rifling through old files, looking for a certain specific one.

He looks dishevelled, unkempt, befuddled.

He is certain he will find them.

He sees fragments of her. Her golden hair against the fading evening light.

A flash of her athletic calves.

Her raucous laugh.

In some distant recess of his brain, he can even hear her.

Her raspy unwomanly voice.

He chuckles at that.

He can even smell the torte she baked, he smacks his lips, drooling a little, the taste of the cake lingering on his tongue.

He begins to call out, but her name gets lost in his mouth.

He simply cannot recall her face.

It's a blank.

He continues scraping, digging, raking.

He knows he will see her.

She is hiding in the most precious corner of his memory.

Graceful, poised and steadfast, she sits beside the man she knew once, only witnessing glimpses of his old self.

She is grateful for those precious moments, brief as they are, when he looks at her with absolute clarity.

She prates on unyieldingly, painstakingly, about their lives together, clasping his old wrinkled hands in hers.

Their pulses beat in perfect rhythm as their love echoes off one another.

TIME

Time flies but it also gets trapped for eternity in memories. We take a pick of those to get by.

Wrapped in memories and her warmest shawl, she sat on her porch.
Her feeble bent frame, crouched insignificantly in the large rocking chair.
The scratched surface and the chipped wood,
resonated a camaraderie of years.

Her wrinkled, sagging yellowed skin,
a shared kinship with her fragile geriatric friends,
her books.
Their spines frayed and delicate like hers.
Their pages brittle like her bones.

The deep blue trunk with dented edges,
the only precious treasure she owned.
Encasing her life,
sat perched beside her.
Unstable, a remnant of itself,
like she was.
It had quietly become old with her.

Her crooked fingers cradle a pair of memoirs,
hand written.
Reminiscent of the ink-stained fingers and smooth flow of her Parker pen.
Her face warms to the memories,
and a toothless smile lights up her face.
She can smell it.
The odour of motherhood.
It has memories of her unsure and faltering steps as she had held her babies nervously.
Of failures, many, many, many failures and learning (which was a never-ending process).
Of never being able to have her heart beat for herself alone.

How she had wanted to stop time at the first tinkly, gurgle of laughter.
She had contorted her facial features and pumped her arms up and down, squawking.
He'd been delighted.
He'd discovered laughter.

Her son, all of 3 months old.

She remembers repeating her silly antics just so the mirth would never stop.

She still remembers the colour of the sky.

It matched her son's outfit that day.

It now lay in her trunk safely, enveloping the warmth of the sun and the turquoise of the sky.

The florid satin ribbons, lying curled in a corner, like a captured rainbow, still smelt of those auburn curls.

She giggled at the sight of the wee shoes. They had stored all the laughter of the day when her little girl had donned them. Footwear confused her. This pair had her walking cautiously, each step deliberate and utterly comical.

The sight of the sipper still redolent with tanginess made her chuckle at the memory of the grimacing face when her daughter had her maiden taste of orange juice.

She smiled, she cried.

Breathing in love.

She sat cuddling her life.

Her eyelids heavy with sleep,

she lay dreaming, ensconced in a world that was.

A world they grew out of and she into.

The sky lit up with the mild orange and gold of the setting sun,

and her time.

DEAR GOD

Far.
Far away,
from the,
cacophony of cries carried by the wind,
pained and frenzied.

Far from the sound of breaking hearts and silent tears.

From this world of conditions, ifs and buts.

I want to curl up in the palm of your hands and sleep.

DOLL

A doll,
a porcelain doll.
Delicate and fragile.
A decorative to flaunt.
A curio on a mantle.
With a master.
To do his bidding.
Sit, stand,
dance, speak,
laugh, cry,
die.

Broken
and smashed.
And then put together,
with gentle care and finesse.

The cracks as scars remain.

The master calls it love.

COFFEE

My cup of coffee drowns my woes in it.

She takes my sloppy dishevelled self and exchanges it with her (I like to think of coffee as a 'she') sharp wit, alertness and happy quotient.

We are a couple in a strange way.

Cannot be apart.

One of us gets cranky.

JOY

Joy likes to surprise you.

It comes to visit in sometimes unusual settings.

It brings gladness of heart in the simplest of ways.

Some moments leave an everlasting impression, sort of washing over you and lingering there like a sweet aftertaste of a favourite dessert.

It bubbles up inside and brings about the warmest sensation from the depths of your heart.

Smiling is involuntary.

A man in tatters, threadbare clothes barely hanging on his body, barefoot, unwashed, probably diseased, not a penny to his name, sits by the road with his yellowing chipped teeth, laughing the most honest laugh, gaiety echoing off him.

I watch delightedly as he sits cuddled with another of his kind but of a different species. Both share tea from a precious three-inch-tall plastic container.

The cup appears to overflow with love, happiness and comradery just perfectly right for the two of them.

A rickshaw puller, strong limbed, muscles taut and toned, perhaps awaiting a customer, tires of his rickshaw seat and decides to assist traffic.

Guides vehicles, urging the movement of the mechanical throng. The two designated policemen are grateful for a little respite.

At one point, this man in worn-out, paper-thin slippers, aids a nervous woman manoeuvre her car into a parking spot.

Her teensy child all of perhaps six years, doesn't forget her manners, smiles and mouths a 'thank you'.

The widest grin is plastered across the man's face and his arm continues to wave at the child long after she has walked off.

That was the face of unfettered happiness.

A snarl of traffic, aggressive and dominating, hogging the road, speeding, not letting up.

Each human obsessed with the aim of getting to their destination in terribly impatient haste.

Standing on one side is a young man who looks like everyone else but he really isn't.

He is standing looking to the other side at a helpless canine who simply cannot map his way between the vehicles to cross the road.

This certain young man who is different because he has a heart of gold. He goes right up to this dog and carries him across the road.

There is a certain roadside shack, an eatery. It's seldom vacant and on most days boasts of topping the popularity chart.

The patronage includes all the labour class from around the upcoming posh apartment buildings and all of the street canine squad.

They sit in perfect harmony, both man and animal slaking their thirst and appetite. Satiated in equal measure with food and company.

The accompanying music playing on an ancient radio only enhances the ambience.

It's a place that can pride itself at having the largest heart.

Kindness is the universal language which does not need 'word crutches'. Just a warm hug, an understanding nod, and small gestures of love and humanity.

THE BELIEVER

Musty, the smell of sadness and old age. Somehow her home always hosted this odour. The structure itself seemed to sag. Burdened with its own weight. Forlorn and desolate. It looked hunched over and tired. Like a man who had aged before his time.

The insides, a pristine white. The walls painted in purity. She couldn't overcome the overwhelming feeling of it being painted in sorrow. She only saw a dull ochre, the colour sadness would embody if it took form. The dank, dark smell of illness and ill luck always seemed to be lurking, biding its time. Alert to the slightest hint of happiness, the woes would seep in, sly and sneaky, wafting in like a light breeze but heavy as lead once settled in. Stubborn and clingy.

There was always a sense of unfinished business as if the house was edgy with a lingering sense of frustration.

The first time she heard the muted whimpering, she dismissed it as a figment of her fertile imagination, much endorsed by her mother. Her ability to communicate with creatures of species other than her own was interpreted as a manifestation of loneliness brought on by having been a single child.

Unbeknownst to her parents, Aisha continued to be deeply involved with the animal kingdom, almost like a mentor.

The next time, the whimpering was distinct, determinedly demanding her attention. The mild snivelling, took the form of loud sobs. They were the cries of a woman in deep distress. The entire room echoed with the piteous weeping. Completely befuddled, she tried frantically to seek out the source, calling out, cajoling. She desperately wanted to help. It then took on a frenzied form, with the cries changing from moaning to bawling, to an angry outburst, to anguished mewling. Then as abruptly as it had begun, it simply stopped. Her room became airless. Silent like a tomb. A chilly gust whooshed past her, whispering in her ear, a wish, a secret.

Aisha, saw the dog instantly as she approached the dishevelled, unkempt area with overgrown grass. The house behind, a picture of complete abandonment. Once an architectural delight, it was utterly derelict, dilapidated, a building in ruins, without a soul.

The dog lay still as in death. His fur scraggly and flea infested, his body a bag of bones. But miraculously he was alive. His breathing was shallow, laboured and he struggled to take in air. He seemed to have no will to live.

When Aisha gently lifted his head and placed it on her lap, the dog knew. Tears streaming down her face, she whispered softly in his ears, his eyes flickered briefly and he howled with unimaginable pain and hurt. Gently she gathered his frail form and took him home.

As she painstakingly nursed him, each day, her house began to breathe, almost heaving a sigh of relief. It seemed to stand taller. It glowed with sunshine. The insides blossomed with a rainbow of colours. The walls shone with pride. A chaste, peaceful white.

The first spring brought on a riot of flowers around. Fresh green leaves glistening in the sunlight. Teal blue skies full of hope. The first rain washed away all the hopelessness. The house smelt of sunshine and the oceans.

Happiness had a scent. The redolence of joy. The odour of life.

IRONY

Born into the privileged lineage, of the keepers of *Dharma.*
The learned ones,
the consecrated ones,
ordained by God himself,
created in his very image.
To uphold societal sanctity,
and preserve morality.
Custodians of the purity of the kosher soul.

She was the epitome of human supremacy.
Elite aristocracy wrapped in casteism.
That haughty arrogance.
The hubris.

Her first born,
the carrier,
of the inheritance.
Of the chaste genes.
He was the guardian of the *Vedas, Puranas.*
He was the embodiment of the holy scriptures.

He was,
defiant and common,
a pagan to her dogmas.
He believed,
he knew of men,
with the goodness of God.

Embraced those that were shunned.
He could not deny another human,
dignity.
Ousted and disinherited by his own.
He knew of no greater blessing.

Like blanched tomatoes, that's how his mother's skin looks like now.
Delicate, brittle like rice paper.

He is afraid to touch her.
She is fragile, just like her ego once.
Her bones, hollowed and porous.
A hug would break her.
She had become 'untouchable'.

HOW TO LOVE RIGHT

All we seek is love. Often left broken hearted or disillusioned. Perhaps we don't look in the right place.

Women cannot be made to order. Life is not a rhyming poem. Everyone and everything is flawed. Just like this unrhyming piece.

Love me for who I am,
with my imperfections and scars.
Inside out.

Whatever I am.
Whoever I choose to be.
I want you to let me be me.
If you want me to change,
then, I will not be me.
I need my dignity,
that resilience.
I have a voice, I need to use.

There are enough of us,
playing parts,
being whoever, we are expected to be.
How then are we different from clay?

I need you to let me be me.
Just me.
Only then can I love you too.

SAY SOMETHING

Emotions need an outlet.
Else, they make a pile like bricks,
with resentment and suppressed feelings as cement.

This is one wall which will not collapse easily.
Talk, argue, discuss.
Open up with all those you care about.
Love always finds a way.

Talk about what makes you sad.
Talk more about what makes you happy.
For what you are grateful.

Communication is the highest form of intimacy and friendship.

PROMISES

Before the alphabet jostles around,
to form words,
there are thoughts.
The link between you and your conscience.
Thoughts,
that course through your heart, soul and mind,
forming, erasing, phrasing.

Words are powerful,
and meaningful.
Sometimes,
they are professed as promises.
Promises are sacred.
Promises should be wrapped in silk,
and kept safe.
Because,
in this heartless world,
some people, still hold onto trust and faith,
for whatever its worth.
Some people take promises seriously.

WHAT'S LOVE GOT TO DO WITH IT

The saddest kind of loneliness is when you feel it amidst your own.

Is it love,
when, the one you love,
can't feel your love?

Is it love,
when,
you can hear his thoughts,
before they become words.
Feel his heart beat in yours.
When,
he looks at you but the language of your eyes,
evades him.
He doesn't know that your heart is incapable of beating alone.

Is it love,
When,
he throws his head back
and laughs,
and you feel light headed.
Your happiness coming through his.
When,
you seek refuge,
from your sadness,
behind your smile.
He cannot see the broken spirit behind the squared shoulders.

Is it love,
when,
the pristine rays of the morning sun,

wash over him, turning him to gold,
and your hand,
with unsure fingers, yearns to caress,
his sculpted features.

When,
your fragmented soul seeks,
answers,
when broken vows and faith lay strewn like shards of glass.

Is it love,
when,
it is moody and porous.
And guilty of dishonesty and deception.
Fluctuating in its impermanence.

Is it love,
when,
the one you love, cannot feel your love.

BLAME IT ON THE NAME

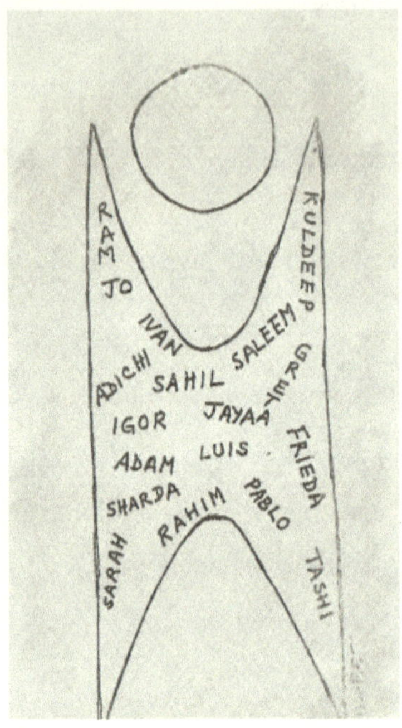

A man named 'X' ate beef.

It was permissible by his religious edict but not by another's, so he was simply slaughtered (along with the ingested 'holy' cow).

A man named 'Y' ate pig.

It was within his religious parameters.

No one has killed him yet.

He is, however, a sitting duck.

A few others named, 'A', 'B', 'C', simply eat just about anything that suits their fancy.

Their religion is probably a varied cuisine!!

This kind, maybe, confuses the others, so, they remain safe.

Logically, if you can eat another life, be it an elephant or an ant and everything in between, religion should not really be the guiding light.

I don't think 'God' would approve of a killing for gastronomic pleasure anyway.

So, here's the thing, it's the,
'Name' to blame.

I do not wish to be known by a name,
the onus of which, on my father's shoulders lain.
A name, that distinguishes me from another human.
I do not want to belong, to a tribe or a clan,
I wish to be a pagan.

Names are chasms,
abysses and pits of darkness.
They are a portent of irreconcilable rifts,
catastrophic wars,
and heart wrenching cruelties.
They are the reason for massacres and delusional superiorities.

My name should be for me to own,
to demean or cast a slur on.
Or,
to uphold and maintain sacred.

HOW TO LIVE AFTER YOU DIE

The most vivid and bewildering memory of the instant your world, as you knew it, comes crashing down is the ordinariness of the moment.

You wonder how everything around you is in order. Every part of you seems disconnected from you, as if your entire being has been blown to smithereens. Like a land that lays in the aftermath of a bomb blast. Ruined. All that remains is the debris. You lie strewn all over. Your mind cannot assimilate or comprehend the magnitude of it all.

This is how it would feel if a bus hit you maybe. Till it hits you, you have no idea how much it would hurt. How it would knock the life out of you as you lie splayed trying to breathe, trying to stay alive.

You want to collect yourself together, collect all the scattered pieces of you and put them together. Like trying to assemble a favourite precious vase that broke. You want to put it back and somehow make it whole like it used to be. But you cannot mend a broken heart or vase. The cracks always show.

It's surreal. It's almost as if it isn't you but someone else. Or it's a terrible nightmare and you will simply wake up.

There are sounds of laughter, some banter.

Traffic moves like it's just another ordinary day.

The sun shines bright sparkling in all its glory, the sky glows a peaceful blue, as if all is right with the world. You on the other hand have no clue about the direction your life will take. Everything has lost its place and meaning.

Birds chirp gaily flitting about, cooing sweet nothings to one another, squirrels scurry up and down branches, noisy and persistent, street dogs come by wagging their tails, vendors go about selling their goods.

These sights make me nauseous. Angry. It's like the world doesn't give a farthing about my state of demolition, I'm inconsequential, a speck, a nobody. Dispensable. Like a disposable glass. Used, thrown and forgotten.

The Sun's light just seems wrong. The trees stand determinedly steadfast, my agony has not shaken them. They stand rooted while I'm uprooted and flung miles away from my foundation. Plants stretch and reach out to the golden orb breathing in life as mine seems to ebb away.

And you begin to hate the world. You want to tear it down just like your insides were. You want to rip it apart with your nails.

You want to scream till you have no scream left.

You want to disappear. You want the earth to split open and swallow you.

You want to die. But then you don't. You don't die. You don't disappear. You get up and you live.

You live for those you love.

There is extraordinary power in responsibility. There is extraordinary power in the love for your children. There is extraordinary power in the ordinary.

It will always save you.

MIRROR! MIRROR!

Do you think even you,
know you?
Delve in and look deep.
Look in the mirror.
Is it you?
Or just someone you keep.
To metamorphose into the roles you play.
Ask around,
hear what people say.
Do they all know the same you?

NRITYA

When,
what beats as your pulse, is rhythm,
what flows in you is music.
When,
the sensation of the *ragas*,
envelops your being.

When,
your feet tap unbeknownst to you,
your hands mould and meld into *mudras*,
and your soul shines through your eyes.

When dancing is the only love you feel,
and you glow with this emotion.

When you are *Radha*,
and sway to Krishna's flute, enraptured and enslaved with his magic.
Unabashedly, revelling in his love.

When,
you are *Shiva*,
and the *Tandava* is your liberation,
your salvation.

When,
you are *Parvati*,
delicate, sensual and graceful.

When this is your *Nirvana*.

When *Raga*, *Vadya* and *Nritya* are you.

Only then,
and,
only when no one can tell you and your dance apart, can you call yourself a dancer.

HOPE

It was over.

Just like that.

Unexpected.

This time it had been easy.

Almost five decades of something she could not give a name to or explain.

She stood numb.

Her heart constricted.

Breathing laboured.

Isn't this what she had yearned for?

Her obsession.

Her freedom.

Her salvation.

The weight of sadness, of years and years,
descended upon her.
As if a dam finally gave away,
succumbing to the violent turbulence of water.

Her legs seemed to crumble,
and her frail frame felt cumbersome.
Her hands,
busy hands,
useful hands,
lay futile,
limp, empty.

A vestigial part of her body.

Her eyes bereft,
exhausted hollows,
desiccant.
Wrinkles like ravines ran riot,
reminiscent of the course of her angst.
Her soul shredded and torn,
lay collapsed and beaten.

Only,
with the familiar gentle embrace,
did her cold body begin to feel,
a spark of life.

The steady, strong hands,
shaped just like hers,
long tapering fingers,
a broad palm,
protruding veins.
Dependable.
Helped her find her feet.
Held her up.

Looking into those steeled eyes,
she knew she could live again.

Together,
she and the one,
born from her heart,
began to walk towards love, faith and hope.

HOME

Splayed,
across her bed,
she felt spent and worn.

Nestled in her cosy cocoon, she lay listlessly.
Movement of any kind was agonising.
Immobile, inert.
She could be mistaken for a corpse.

Only,
in her head was,
a storm of wild emotions,
whirring away relentlessly,
mercilessly.

The familiar ache,
had returned.
Intense and physical.
The longing acute.
Unforgiving.
Gnawing.
She could bear it no longer.

With Herculean effort,
she willed her lifeless body, into action.
She knew what she had to do,
to, breathe and to feel her heart beat again.

At the threshold,
she stood.
Wrapped in a wave of nostalgia.
Her tired, hungry eyes wanted to capture everything in her sight.
Devour all of it,
and keep it.
Hide it away.
It was hers,
and hers alone.

With teetering and staggering steps,
she plodded forward.
With quivering hands,
she unlatched the rusted eroded door.

The smell overwhelmed her.
It was still there.
The unmistakable odour of home.
Hidden, inconspicuous and shy.
But she would recognise it, amidst a million others.

Her eyes travelled around,
and locked away the images behind her eyelids.
It was unchanged, yet changed.
Reminiscent of her life that was.

Now covered with the dust of time.
Every part echoed with what was.
Every room had safely stored away memories for her,
a secret happy stash,

She laughed.
And she cried.
She traced patterns on the canvas of dust.
Her trailing fingers layered with the past.

The sudden rain,
came as a soothsayer
an augur.
Of an end to pain.

She stood under the growling clouds,
her being infused with ambrosia.
She swallowed the raindrops,
and a rainbow formed on her heart.

She sat in the lap of her faithful tree,
an old reliable, steadfast friend.
She nestled in his roots.
She seemed to grow out of it.
Her arms merging with the branches,
her hair blowing with the leaves in the wind.

The sun began to glow out of her.
Her eyes brimmed,
and overflew into the river.

This was where she belonged.
This is where her soul had lived.
Over and over.

ON KASHMIR

Kashmir tugs at my heart.

The vicious circle of strife.
The inane loss of precious lives,
lives reduced to mere statistics.
The absolute abuse of her being.

Yet, she sits strong.
She flaunts her beauty.
And she is generous.
Almost challenging the orchestrators of violence.

This feeling of utter helplessness has only grown, as has the irretrievably complicated situation in Kashmir.

I have spent the best years of my life in the lap of her altruism.
During the heady throes of my youth.
When idealism was the order of the day and one believed.
When the world was quite an extraordinary place full of hope and joy.

That utterly naïve and idyllic age when you felt you could make a difference.

The breath-taking beauty and aura of Kashmir was guilty of adding to this delusion.

Every breath of the pure unadulterated air was taken for granted.

The magnanimous fruit orchards whose generosity never ebbed.

One could just pluck crisp fresh apples and crunch on them whilst ambling along the Dal Lake.

We feared no one and were free as the birds.

The vast viridian, an expanse so massive, one didn't know where it started or ended.

As children, we only knew how exhilarating it was to run unfettered across these capacious meadows.

We never knew of boundaries or divisions in hearts.

Even the extreme winter brought magic.

We would be waiting, with our noses pressed against the window panes, to catch sight of the first snowflake.

Then rush outside to taste them, our frozen tongues sticking out with not a care in the world.

The imperfect snowmen,

quite unlike those in the movies or comic books, but snowmen they were nonetheless.

The snowballs flung at unsuspecting victims.

We had our own Switzerland.

The winter never felt bitter.

We were engulfed in the warmth of *kehwa*,

and the love of our local neighbours.

The cold sashayed into delightful spring bringing a gentle warmth, turning the landscape into a spectacular potpourri of colours.

What a magnificent array of blossoms and birds.

It was all too intoxicating.

Kashmir has been too giving. Her generosity has made us humans more human,

jealous, possessive, selfish.

The kind of affinity I feel, am sure pales in comparison to those who had homes, who knew nothing better than Kashmir. I cannot even begin to imagine the angst they feel. It's not about the brick constructions called houses.

It's about memories,

in being born,

breathing,

building lives,

making homes,

It's about roots.

It's about security.

It's about identity.

Kashmir gets into your system and stays, just as the camaraderie amongst the common people; regardless of political chasms created by the destroyers of peace.

According to a certain line of thought, humans speak about things that do not exist.

It's commonly called gossip.

This fact struck home while reading a book called 'Sapiens'.

The author states, that we collectively weave myths, and tend to believe in them.

This is true only for humans.

The author hits the nail on the head with the following example.

You cannot convince a monkey to be your slave or avow undying loyalty by promising him limitless bananas after death in monkey heaven!!

Fiction can take a dangerous turn as it has in strife ridden areas.

Most of these are created for political motives which are impossible to fathom or unravel.

If only the collective in Kashmir would be more like the monkeys...!!!

MEMORY BANK

There is something about smells.
They really are, simply put, memory banks.
Turgescent and smug with their secret stash.
Portals to time travel.
Vaults of magic,
that make you feel warm, fuzzy and safe.

A certain perfume,
reminds me, of my innocent yearning,
of wanting to grow up.
So, I could smell like mum,
and wrap myself in six yards of enigma.

My old coat is a treasure trove,
of fancy dreams,
of secrets,
of friendships.
I often bury my nose,
in it, to inhale happiness.

I sometimes catch a whiff of Kashmir,
in the glowing embers of coal.
A story, in the breath of a passing breeze.

A hint of Chinar,
on a cold, grey, winter day,
smells of the last snatches,
of the, coveted naivety of my childhood.

Cinnamon and almond,
carries the aroma of blossoming love,
with my first taste of *Kehwa*

The tangy redolence of apples,
the sweet fragrance of blossoms,
the woody, strong and earthy scent of the forest,
simple and pure,
tinged with a hint of pine essence,
resonates with the easy laughter of my children.
Our leisurely strolls to nowhere in particular.
Just us.
And nature.
A balm for our invisible sores.

Beneath my eyelids, is stored an album.
Of memories.
The pages flip,
and send me cascading across time spans,
at the mere hint,
of a certain scent.

LETTERS

Was it the morning or the evening post?
My memory blurs at this trifling detail.
Has my brain become feeble?
An insignificant symptom of a significant ailment?
My impeccable memory,
("How do you remember birthdays and anniversaries?")
is showing frailty.
Just like us.

But I reminisce,
almost, like a masochist.
Those days, are etched in my head, stubborn and steadfast.
I clutch fiercely, possessively,
at what was.

The wait.
The anticipation.
the stoic act,
the art of nonchalance.

But, if my heart were ripped apart,
there'd be a volcanic eruption.

My heart,
beating so wild,
I could barely contain it!
Shushing it wouldn't help really.
I could hear it in my ears.

The firmly glued envelope,
the only hindrance,
between you and me.
Frantic tearing,
then reading,
and dreaming and dreaming.

You my dearest one,
seldom disappointed me.
Oh, it was magical.
And what a sorcerer you were.
Eros himself.
Words woven around my soul, intricately,
beautifully.
Enchanted and enmeshed,
I was a prisoner insatiated.

Every word sacrosanct.
Love sacrosanct.
It was religion beyond mortal comprehension.
You owned me.

Your letters possessed me.
Words that spun dreams,
of clasped hands,
of entwined souls,
of one breath,
of hearing your heart beat in mine,
of this love being our only language.
Yours and mine.
Words to hold our love as a shrine.

Oh, those tricksters,
dream weavers,
those letters.

What artful chicanery.
So, they had to be my nemesis.
Those letters.
Read and reread.
Lived and relived.

Filed away.
Emotions filed away.
Life filed away.

Precious possessions.
Mere promises.
Only words.
Letters strung into words.
Tacit words within the written.
Unheard, unseen.

Dusty love.
Forgotten love.
Chronicled love.
My love.

Those are what I burnt today.
They were occupying too much space in my heart.

GOD, PLEASE SHOW YOURSELF

The only thing that stands between Man and God is Religion.

Religion needs to keep up with the times. Just like Apps, it needs to be updated, without which it would crash.

The world is on the verge of moral collapse owing to the archaic nature of certain edicts.

Since time immemorial, religion and power (kings, lords etc.) have functioned hand in glove. Each keeping the other safe, a mutual sustenance, for more reasons, than evident.

This lethal combination has over centuries, systematically and cunningly destroyed humanity.

Religion has become an ugly word. It's the most vicious face of politics. It stirs up the vilest thoughts, initiates the most vehement and mindless violence.

Loss of young able lives, brainwashed into insane beliefs.

We have the most trying and unusual ways of exhibiting our faith and allegiance to the supreme;

Casteism, gender bias, racism, blaring *'Bhajans'* or a discourse which you do not listen to because you are frantically trying to prevent hearing damage.

Large processions on highways, busy streets.

And now killing too.

How simple it is to slaughter another human for reasons that are becoming eerily ludicrous.

Your diet;

Attire;

Language;

Anything could get you killed in the name of the Almighty.

Period.

I don't know how many of us feel pious?

How can faith and fear be on the same plate?

Terrorism and God?!!

How can any religion profess, justify and uphold
murder as a means to achieve God?

If so, it's high time God made his presence felt.

We need an explanation.

Religion does not seem to work for mankind, perhaps Atheism would.

I'd rather be a part of a society of pagans wherein being humane is the only Religion.

WORLDS APART

I had a wish.
My wish was you.
I knew you.
I knew your smell.
I had seen you,
before you became you.

You were me,
I was you.
You were my breath,
you coursed through me,
like a river,
over my arid, parched soul.
I had kissed you,
every part of you,
before you became you.

Your whispers,
snug and safe in my ears.
I had heard you,
before you became you.
I had carried you,
you, the weight of love.
I floated,
light as air, while you,
you nestled in a curl, secure in your cove.

In another world,
when you became you,
We met at another level.
We were two now,
you and I.

Years slipped through my fingers,
like water.
In this world,
you built spaces,
and voids,
my love could not fill.

In this world,
of needs and wants,
of conditions;
each with its limitations.
Love was at a loss.

In this world,
of borrowed time,
and impermanence,
of all that is real and true,
my love,
for you,
became a burden to bear.

•••

RIB TICKLERS

Nothing is more therapeutic than a hearty laugh.

PTV (PRE-TEEN TEEN VIRUS)

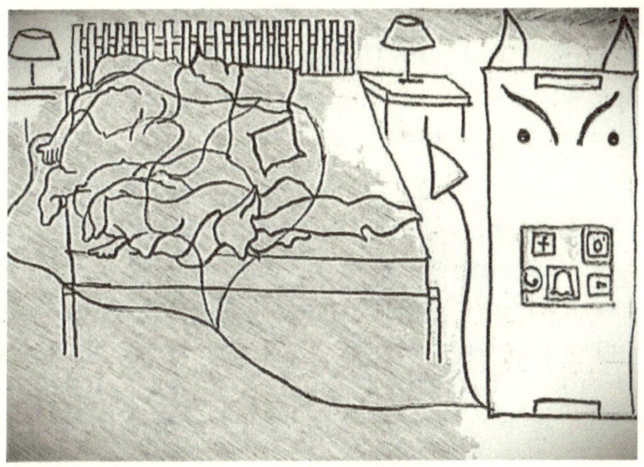

Usually begins to afflict children at ages of 10 and onwards. Symptoms include,

Inability to wake before at least noon.

Inability to sleep before 3 a.m.

Extreme lethargy which makes it very painful for children to raise their limbs to throw trash in the bin placed half an inch away from their bed. (Chocolates, chips, chewing gum wrappers, empty soft drink bottles, tissues etc).

This sense of fatigue also demands room service and the unwashed breakfast, lunch, dinner dishes lie strewn till the attendant (mostly mother) collects them.

This feeling of death in mobility also results in a terrible confusion regarding clothes. Of not knowing whether they are extending and flowing out from the cupboards or into them. There are categories to them; the clean, not so clean and definitely, horribly dirty and needing a quarantined wash with Dettol. They all lie in sad mangled heaps. Any attempt at collecting them or organising them is excruciating for the ailing child.

The virus affects communication with parents in a strange way. Conversations are in the form of frowns, grunts, raised eyebrows and animated hand gestures. Speech becomes limited to a kind of slurry drawl with the use of words that sound like an alien language. It is rather frightening because the guardians begin to imagine the worst having spent so much time, effort and moolah on the offspring's education. This sudden impairment in speech, in forming sentences and having coherent conversations is quite perplexing. Adding further to this befuddled state is finding the child prating hours on end with his/ her beau.

God forbid if the child gets a secondary infection called 'falling in love'. Every one, everything, falls along with. The brain simply short-circuits. The child hallucinates, sees kaleidoscopic colours, begins to develop a 'profound' understanding of quotes and poetry. Likes to remain in a room not touched by sunlight, encouraging the longevity of the affliction.

The virus is truly evil. It instigates terrible tantrums, Hulk like stomping, door slamming (most homes with teens have doors hanging on sheer will power), eye rolling, the desire to play nerve racking, eardrum shattering, earthquake like vibration causing supposed music which is an amalgamation of instruments with a special preference to drums and scratchy guitar playing, with 'singer(s)' who sound like they are at war or they suffer from some terrible throat disease. The lyrics??? Well never mind!

This is one ghost you cannot exorcise!

You will begin to also notice that the clothes will become threadbare, and no, it's not in solidarity with the poor. Apparel just hangs loose or begins at the lowest point of the waist, at the edge of the derriere and falls into a crumpled heap at the ankles. How it stays where it does is a miracle. The hair is uncombed. The walk is a mix of a swagger and apelike ancestral stance.

The virus embeds itself and works in very mysterious ways.

One of the stages of the progression of this ailment is an extreme attachment to the mobile phone. It seems to be a life-giving medium which has its invisible tentacles embedded in all the vital organs of its victim. I have a nagging suspicion that it sucks out life instead.

There is just breathing space between the gadget and the patient. Eyes agog, rapt, sometimes one hears somewhat manic sniggers and titters interspersed with exclamations of various emotions. It's a sad spectacle. A human interacting with a machine on a one-to-one basis.

There is NO antidote, vaccine or cure.

Only time, time heals!!

It's impossible for children and adults to escape it.

It's imperative that a little booklet of instructions be circulated amongst all potential, susceptible victims.

"Issued in the general interest of the public!!"

THE 'MOTHER' TONGUE

Me ordering burgers from****

After a prolonged ring, I am greeted by a very American voice guiding me to press various buttons.

"Gooodevaning****dalivaaryIam….(a name I cannot for the life of me understand) haomayIhalpyoo?"

Am sure all the recruits at ****undergo rigorous *Pranayama* (breathing exercise) during training!

I ask if I can place my order.

After confirming my mobile number, the gent proceeds to accept the order,

Man: OK Mr Pooja, vaatvudyoolaiktoaader?

Me: Uh..er..Just a minute.

I move the mobile from my ear, look towards the kids and ask if (over the years spent yelling at them) I have begun to sound like a man!!

Kids: (Synchronised shrug)...Maybe!!!

They leave the room to guffaw in private. The joke is on me.

Back to ordering.

Me: I would like to order Q, R, S, T, U, V, X, Y, Z burgers. (It's a large order because the kids want the lot to last until breakfast and I am not complaining).

Man: So, Ma'am, Sir, yoovudlaiktodaliverthaarder?

Me: No! YOU will deliver and I will order.

Man: YaasmemMrPooja.

At this point I suggest to him that I am perfectly comfortable with Hindi. Almost relieved, he switches eagerly and the ensuing conversation is comprehensible to both.

Confirming the order however, the great language comes back into action wherein he insists on emphasising that the chicken burgers are 'non-vegetarian' and the paneer ones vegetarian!!'

Two toddlers, standing tall at perhaps two feet nothing, out for an evening stroll.

One accompanied by his granny and the other by young house 'help'.

Granny wanting to initiate friendship for her grandson asks the other little fellow,

"Beta aapka kya naam hai?" (What is your name, son?)

Kiddo twists his torso left, right, turns his feet in, digs his heels in, raises and swings his arms.

House help comes to the rescue, says "Ye Heendee nai bolta hai (he does not speak Hindi).

"Aah" says the granny.

Rephrases her question, "Beta vaat eez yer name?"

Kid puts his little hands together, entwining his tiny fingers, smiles coyly and obliges the old lady with one.

ON VANITY

Sometimes, mirrors lie.

Vanity is not my cup of tea.

Most days, I don a pair of cotton shorts with an oversized Tee. I'd recommend wearing and washing them often, for enhanced comfort.

Of course, to go with, rubber slippers make sense, right?!

And short hair is really cool, you don't even need to use a comb!!
Just a run through with your fingers works perfectly.

I am absolutely mortified with the idea of using any kind of beauty enhancers, the catch word here is 'beauty'.
I'm not sure I have any 'enhanceable' assets anyway.

It's mind-boggling, the array of products that promise you eternal youth.
There seems to be something and something more in that something, for every part of the little face one has.
Guess the face can accommodate a lot more than one would imagine!

I am sure I must have been a huge disappointment to my very stylish in-laws (they must wonder if their, then, very eligible boy did not really suffer from a temporary bout of insanity to have wanted to be betrothed to this wild creature!).

They tried,
in the early years,
when hope hadn't died.
Face wash, face pack, face scrub, face....
"Face it (I was told).
You need it.
Try it.
You will glow.
Oh! and do get work on your brow!"

I nodded and agreed.
Disagreed!
Evaded and avoided the deed!

But!
One day,
I got caught.
Off to a salon I was sent,
to get a magical redoing of my face.
Greeted at the entrance,
by a cardamom chewing,
Bollywoodsong humming,
layered lipstick (yes blood red in colour) wearing,
smiling lady.
She was 'Cruella' from 101 Dalmatians!
On a cold metallic table, I was lain,
not unlike the one in an operation theatre,
so, I worried about who else had lain or was slain.
To be worked upon from toe to hair.
My OCD kicking in just then,
but the ordeal had only just begun.

Wet towels were brought in. (Oh no! I couldn't have a public towel touch my face! Eeeeeeewwww!! Did they have any Dettol?!!).

I was looked at with disdain and then ignored.

This very adept lady, trying to coo incomprehensible beauty benefits began 'uncleaning' my face with gentle circular movements.

I wanted out!!

Was it okay to shout?

Whilst I was strategising my escape,

she came back with some instruments that menacingly looked like a scalpel and a mini cattle prod.

Seriously?!!

Those would not scar my face but make it pretty?

Pretty Scarface!!!

I didn't want to be called that!!

So, I tried sitting up.

"No! No! Madam! Just relax, don't move! Kahin 'sleep' ho gaya toh lag jaaega! Aap tension mat lo, yeh 'sterile' hai!"

"Oh!" I managed to squeak.

I am hoping she was referring to the instruments being sterilised and not the guys sitting in the hair cut cubicle!!

So, she held me down, gently of course and went ahead with what seemed like mining for ore.

Some Bhojbollypuri songs played in the background and the miner lady hummed along happily,

whilst I lay there in catatonic stupor.

The above done,

some cold and sticky goo was slathered up from my neck to my face.

Gaaaaaaaah....!!

She spared my eyes.

Or did she?!!

Surprise!!!

Eye masks in the form of appetising cucumbers were placed,

I wondered if I could eat them!!

Soon my features felt stretched and taut.

I was stuck in my own face!!

Of course, I couldn't speak or move a muscle.

The efficient orchestrator would periodically come and dab around,

smile benignly and say, "abhi thodi der aur", and her humming wouldn't stop!!

Why was she so gleeful?

Finally, what was applied as a soft blob was removed as a caricature of my face!!

I realised I had a pretty weird nose.

Not to mention the cleft chin and sunken eye holes.

I suddenly empathised with my in-laws.

What followed was a fantastic massage, if I did not count the times 'miss scissor hands' (read nails long enough to cut an apple) did not nearly slice my neck off.

I was let off then, with a, “dekho aap ka chehera kitna glow kar raha hai, yeh golden facial hai, aapko every month karna chaiye, skin bhi tight rahega!”

The only tightness I felt was in my chest!!
I scooted to a nice hot bath with a full bottle of Dettol.

I did carry a souvenir back from the parlour.
My face mask.
I was determined to use it well,
to my advantage,
the next time my in-laws had a similar suggestion.

THE BOOK THIEF

There was this latest edition of the Readers Digest, lying abandoned on the ledge right outside my main door.

I reached for it, turned it over, ruffled the pages, looked through the contents, then put it right back, chiding myself for trying to take what wasn't mine.

Every morning for the next three days I would open the door to this temptation, and I would keep to my business of taking Nuts for a walk and back inside.

Then one morning, I discovered it had fallen off the ledge. Almost imploring me to pick it up.

It did look sad; splayed helplessly with its pages fluttering in the wind.

I thought to myself, this one truly needed adoption, the owner clearly did not want it.

Thus, becoming The Book Thief.

QUITE A SPECTACLE - I

There is only one word to describe having poor eyesight.
Frustrating.
Another that follows closely is embarrassing.
Not because of aesthetics,
I couldn't care a farthing!
It's situations where, you are looking for your glasses, without your glasses!

I have frantically turned, literally everything upside down,
yelled at the kids,
dog and maids,
looking for the blasted pair,
whilst they sat perfectly perched,
atop my head!!

I have walked out of shops apologising,
cursing,
because without my crutches,
a transaction was a cryptic haze.
Only to find them later,
dangling merrily,
from a button hole on my shirt!

Of course,
the incredulous expression on the shopkeeper's face is duly explained.

Other times,
you enter a restaurant, known for its delicacies.
And, all you do is,
stare at overlapping letters that seem to be doing a jolly dance.
You may as well be looking at the impossible Chinese script!
You wish the menu could verbalize the exotic cuisine.
Because you forgot,
and it doesn't dangle from any part of your attire,
you actually forgot to tote the evil necessity.

Drinking hot beverages and reading,
that's way too much to ask for.
It's like, driving through a fog.

Your handicap is a real let down,
especially, socially.
As it is, you can't tell man from woman,
with so much gender merging.
What with long hair and unisex garb.

Not to mention,
those you wish to dodge.
You squint and peer,
but, recognition dawns,
only at a foot's distance, and naturally,
it's too late to lam then!!

It's pure acrobatics,
applying eye makeup,
whilst wearing glasses.
You land up looking like a koala bear or someone with a black eye (could come in handy though getting the husband into trouble).

The 3D movie experience, is lamentable.
And utterly dismal.
Should you wear the dammed pair over the other pair,
or under?!!
It takes a while,
to figure it all.

And in the hot summer,
the options aren't too favourable either.
Goggles or spectacles?
You have to choose between being scorched,
or being near blind!

You cannot even take,
sneak peeks,
into your kids' mobiles.
The moment you don your extra appendages,
the game is over.

For me, it's double jeopardy.
Near or far,
everything's a foggy blur.

The first pair of glasses,
has a fine feel.
You imagine you look all scholarly and mentorish.
But it really is all pish posh!!

All you ever do is,
make a complete spectacle of yourself!

QUITE A SPECTACLE - II

Poor eyesight is making it increasingly difficult to differentiate between a toddler (perhaps not on a leash) and a pet dog (most probably on a leash!!)

Fear of a terrible faux pas in the offing!!

Though 'cute' could work for both.

QUITE A SPECTACLE - III

Failing eyesight has more often than not, landed me in terribly embarrassing situations.

I simply cannot afford to remove my glasses and imagine I can manage.

The other day at a car parking lot, I was met with a glare and a threat that involved cops because I was trying to get into a car that 'apparently' wasn't mine. It was the exact blue the husband had opted for, when asked for a colour choice, believing it to be quite unique.

In my befuddled, semivisioned state, I began tugging at all the car doors and forcibly inserting my vehicle key in panic and desperation.

I refused to give up until I was forced to snap out of my delusional state with a rude and harsh tap on my shoulder.

The man was quite gleeful at having accosted a 'car thief'. That too a woman and an aged one at that!! He appeared to be in an 'Aha' moment with his head full of visuals of being photographed with me in handcuffs. He would stand smiling with a bunch of cops lined up on either side. There would be a giant gift cheque certificate taking up all the photographic space. This picture would make the headlines of the local daily. He stood in this dreamlike stupor till his eyes fell back on me.

I must have looked crazed as well with a head of grey hair which had begun to look as confused as me. My incredulous expression of indignation at being held hostage and questioned must have added to the ridiculous situation.

I was quite furious with the boorish lunk and a heated argument about ownership rights over the car ensued. I thought wearing my spectacles at this point would have a certain effect on the ill-behaved gent. I would look fairly scholarly and senior and prove the car was mine.

Naturally I was in thicker soup than I had anticipated. My glasses had done the disappearing act. Thus ensued 10 mins of looking for my glasses without my glasses. Under the car, on the bonnet, tried to open the doors again and failed, tried the boot, failed. The aggrieved man really thought I was a mental case. He kept staring at me in complete amazement.

He was also a man of reasonable intellect perhaps and figured I was looking for my spectacles. He kept pointing to my head and I kept getting more and more infuriated because I thought he was utterly uncouth by calling me loco with gestures. At some point my hand ran over my head and voila! Of course, with restored vision came restored sense.

No amount of explanation proved to the man that I wasn't a burglar or an escapee from the loony bin. He however agreed not to press charges owing to my deranged look and seniority. He left shaking his head in utter disbelief!!

It's bewildering how we manage to fit in more cars than a parking space can accommodate. Just like our population, I guess. Somehow there always seems to be room for more humans and then for more cars.

We had to visit a certain establishment which was packed to capacity. However, the husband managed to manoeuvre and park the car with a certain expertise particular to the people of this region.

Anyhow our work accomplished we headed back with the husband in the lead to extricate the car. As I approached the blue, I realised some guy was reversing straight into our car! Bravely I stood between the attacker and my car. In the background I could hear desperate honking. I kept ignoring it because we Indians honk. This was followed by a loud calling out of my name. Startled I turned around to discover the husband desperately trying to draw my attention a few meters away, also in the assumed differently coloured car!!

At another time, in the heart of a bustling market place, I found myself sitting in the passenger seat with a complete stranger beside me. As I sat down and opened my bag to access the sanitiser, the person in the driver's seat let out a deafening scream and raised his hands. I looked to the right expecting my husband there and naturally I screamed too!! It was a very difficult task to scatter the crowd that had gathered around the darned blue car.

It does take more than a few setbacks to realise the seriousness of one's handicap.

I was to be picked up by the husband from a decided place. I was waiting by the curb and soon spotted the familiar blue.

In order to draw attention, I began walking towards the car, smiling and waving. As the car slowed down, I slapped my head in dismay. It was indeed the familiar blue but a very unfamiliar man in the driver's seat!

He was quite enthusiastic about offering me a lift. I had to decline with the wildest of excuses.

I now have the darned pair hanging around my neck like a noose.

Although maybe we should have picked an uncommon colour.

M.O.M.

"Yo! Sup!?"

"Cool, bro"(high fives follow).

Greetings over and done with.

Now 'cool' is one marvellous word that can encompass a decent part of the lexicon. It could be,

*State of health and wealth;

*Societal hierarchy;

*Awe;

*Surprise;

*School /college environment;

*Relationship with the beau (who could be an ex or a third-time relationship dropout);

*Sometimes even the weather.

It's absolutely magnificent.

Besides, it's cool to use 'cool'.

This generation,

X (possibly because of a labyrinthine relationship record) or

Y (being the indefatigable posers of the dogged question)

Parent: At least look at what your school books look like.

Gen Y: Y?

Parent: Is it some kind of cult or religious ritual to sleep only after 3 am? You should tuck in earlier.

Gen Y: Y?

Parent: You cannot become a connoisseur of alcoholic beverages at 16!!

Gen Y: Y?

This could be an endless list.

However, we may like to address them, they are champions all the way, non pareil.

Us?

Well, we are too garrulous, too much articulation, exhaustive communication.

Whilst we conflab, our offsprings have initiated the onset of great friendships.

It's a world of short and sweet, of acronyms: gtg, lol, rotfl, ikr, idk (although the last one sounds like someone with an onset of a bout of hiccups).

Minimum effort at conversation.

For the uninformed few it's absolutely agonising. Nothing less than a torturous attempt at learning a foreign language with not even an alphabet to start with.

It's coded encryption.

Well, I am devious that way!

Things I have learnt to unlearn, incorporate a new unvocabulary.

I have learnt to untalk.

All from sources such as,

*Eavesdropping on a teen gathering, (of course while pretending to look for something I supposedly dropped);

*Hacking into kids' various social media accounts;

*Sneaking peeks at kids' text messages.

Undeniably,
I am quite the M.O.M. (Master of Management).

BOOKS

The most precious thing I own after the kids are books. (I don't really own the children!) I must admit, they were quite a joy at one time, till they got infected with the 'teen virus'.

There is no cure for it. It has to run its course. Unfortunately, the symptoms last much longer than a mere seven days. This virus could last a lifetime (of the parents).

I can't really cuddle up with them anymore in a rocking chair, for starters. They don't fit into my lap (I could, into theirs but then, that isn't quite the same thing I suppose).

Talk of maintenance!! I cannot even attempt to make a comparison! I am still the boss with books, I get to judge them, they need to please me. Do I really need to spell out the equation with the kids??!!!!

I don't flaunt my collection of books nor am I particularly enthusiastic about lending them. Now, I don't mind flaunting the offspring, maybe someone might want them, briefly or for good.

JUST A MOM

TRRRRRRRINNNNGGGG!!! Damn! The first expletive of the day uttered, I grope wildly for the darned banshee, upsetting a bottle of water in the bargain, making a diving catch at my antique bedside lamp. Phew!

And I haven't even gotten out of bed just yet.

The sun is trying to edge past the cloudy haze, full of smog, almost like a caterpillar pushing out of its cocoon.

Meanwhile, I curse the winter days as I do each year, promising myself to shift to a sunnier, warmer place.

I don my three pairs of socks, two pullovers, two sets of flannel pyjamas (God, I love those, I'd have icicle legs without them), a woollen cap with ear flaps.

All of this will be welcomed with sniggers and titters from my loving family members.

I am the 'bheegi billi', always cold, even in the summer when the AC is at 25 C°.

I glare at the sleeping 'man of the house', still cosily tucked, with a blissful half smile.

He can afford to smile a lot longer than I can.

At that point, I want to pour ice cold water on his head.

Ordinarily, most people don't have such violent thoughts early in the morning.

I am not ordinary.

I feel really evil on a cold winter morning. I tug at the quilt so it's displaced from the tuck under the chin of my husband and make more noise than necessary just getting to the door.

But he is really from the lineage of Kumbhakarna, he just murmurs, turns the other way and snuggles into an even cosier position.

I slam the door hard on my way out.

(I know this will not even cause a break in the snoring man's dream sequence!).

What I have to accomplish is no mean feat, waking two monsters (in the garb of children).

Attempt 1*

Child 1 Room1: I need to find my way into the room, snake my way between clothes, books, chocolate wrappers, water bottles, wires, other electrical gizmos connected in a maze and avoid getting electrocuted.

I survive death of its only kind where the headlines would read, 'Killer football does mother in!!'

So, having successfully completed this obstacle course, I reach the bed and I need to locate my son from amongst an indecipherable mesh of quilt and sheet, I need to find his face!! Okay, so the dog helps here, by emerging from this enigma, giving me a lead.

Me: Get up! It's 6am!

Child 1: Mnngnhggg..mmm..gnh....Yeh.... mmnnhh...

Dog: Can't speak, but, gives me a look of utter disdain and finds his way back into the cave of mystery.

Child 2 Room 2: Aah! I love this girl, how neat her room looks, unlike the pigsty I just visited. It's easy to get to her. There's a catch here though, I have to adopt protective tactics.

I gingerly shake her shoulders and quickly step back, as expected, she flails her arms wildly, grumbling, (when inexperienced, the same arms have inflicted considerable pain on my face and elsewhere).

I repeat the usual of it being time to wake up, keeping safe distance!!

There is no reaction. I repeat myself.

Child 2 stirs, mumbles, asks for 5 minutes more.

"OK" I say.

It's the standard drill every morning.

I then make my way into my den to get to the reason of my sanity.

Having dosed myself sufficiently with black coffee I feel rejuvenated and recharged!!

The usual brain racking on 'interesting' tiffin boxes ensues.

I know neither of the monsters has woken up.

Attempt 2*

Child 1 Room 1:

Me: Please get up, you're already running late.

Child 1: Wriggles out of his nest, nods, stretches.

Child 2 Room 2:

Me: Wake up, wake up! At this rate you will be certainly late

Child 2: Getting up in 2.

(Ten minutes later)

Attempt 3*

Child 1: Room 1

Me: WHAT'S WRONG WITH YOU?!! YOU'LL BE LATE. YOU NEVER SLEEP ON TIME, YOU'RE ALWAYS AT THE COMPUTER. WHAT DO YOU KEEP DOING ALL NIGHT? I AM FED UP OF YOU. I HAVE BEEN TRYING TO WAKE YOU FOR THE PAST HALF HOUR.

Child 1: Chill mom! Why do you scream so much?!

The Dog, I think, just wants me to leave the room.

Child 2: Room 2

Me: YOUR TWO MINUTES AREN'T OVER YET?!! I HAVE TO KEEP RUNNING FROM ONE ROOM TO THE OTHER JUST TRYING TO WAKE YOU UP.

Child 2: Glares with hands over her ears.

Me: If you miss the bus, I am not ferrying you to school.

Half an hour later, a happy husband emerges, the morning hugs follow with the standard winter season dialogue of not being able to find me with my many layered woollens.

I don't feel terribly romantic though.

The dog comes wagging his tail, even smiling at the husband.

After repeated knocks at both doors and threats of having a word with the school counsellor about bad behaviour and complete lack of respect for time, the kids come out still trying to pack their respective bags, me yelling constantly about them having no foresight about being prepared for school the night previous.

All through this the placid Piscean reads his paper and sips his green tea with lemon in a nice sunny corner of the house.

The kids greet him with such respect and happy love, pleasant good mornings and warm embraces are exchanged.

I stand by, scowling.

The dog sits possessively by the man's side (he never comes and sits next to me).

I tell the dog I will not feed him anymore.

He simply looks at the man, who immediately comforts him with the appropriate words.

He then heads to the loo where he will spend another hour undisturbed before he heads out to work.

The kids do miss the bus and I ferry them to school grumbling all the way.

The kids listen to 'Radio One' at an indecent volume, hoping to drown my voice but I continue relentlessly.

I think the kids plug their ears with sheer will power.

So, my words fall on deaf ears.

This is a follow up enhancement over lip synching with me when I scolded them earlier.

Fifteen minutes later, at home, the dog comes bounding to greet me (only because he knows I have the goodies, Monster no 3!).

I fill his bowl with food and wait for the next onslaught in the form of two loud and garrulous maids.

OK, so now with all the above done and over, I have the house to myself. It takes me a while to feel the pleasure, to breathe easy.

I am torn between all the things I could possibly do.

All I do is miss the kids.

THE INHERITANCE

Chotu, Phunty, Dot, Rumplestiltskin, Four Feet Nothing, Miniature, Shortie;
are just some endearments attributed to me,
for a 'larger' part of my life.

That, kindergarten was where I remained,
well into twelfth grade.
Having to endure cheek pulling,
coochie cooing and mollycoddling.
Till I spouted out a series of high-sounding words.
"It's diabolical!
It's preposterous!
My academic prowess is,
far more advanced than my microscopical stature!"
I had to work on my vocabulary!!
Not that it helped.
I was still subjected,
to unbearable osculation,
being smothered by affection.

I also thought,
opposites, in the way they were taught,
was in poor taste.
I was always tiny, short and small.
The glory belonged to the big and tall!!

My advantaged peers,
boogied to the Beatles,
at morning assembly.
Meanwhile,
a picture of reverence and faith is what I would portray.
Leading the motley crew,
obviously,
because, beyond a couple of feet I never grew!

My conviction, bigger than my frame,
blamed my pigtails for my cuteness quotient.
So, I traded them for the then, 'boy cut'.
Of course, that is precisely what I was constantly mistaken for,
a boy.
A cute boy!!

Marriage was another storey!
Also, story!!
Before I was ceremonially betrothed,
I had the honour, to shake the hand,
and make the acquaintance,
of the epitome of charisma,
General Sam Manekshaw!!

Hearing of my imminent matrimony,
he eyed my father suspiciously,

and accused him of abetting the nuptials,
of a child!
I was twenty-two.

The man of my dreams,
is three of me put together vertically,
now, equally horizontally!!
Guess,
it worked to his advantage,
to have me,
look up to him, all my life.

Amongst the many 'joys' of
being a near dwarf,

Being refused services,
at certain establishments,
because I was 'unaccompanied' by an adult.
My most 'adult' scowl had little effect.
I was waived off as a spoilt brat!!

Upon, introduction as the spouse,
of the tall hunk,
at various social dos,
the travel of the line of eye,
took quite a fall, splat, plunk!!
"Aah! there you are!

Dear me! almost missed you!!
What a little darling you are!"
So much for social confidence!

I have perfected the art,
of ladylike posture,
feet crossed beneath,
tips of my toes gently grazing the floor.
Elegance?!!
Nah!
I seldom find a seating arrangement,
where my feet,
touch the ground!!

Attempts at seriously reprimanding the children,
turns into a comedy show comparable to the ones with high TRPs.
They pretend not to hear me, since they are so high up!!
Whacking them is a game of dodge, I jump to smack and they deftly evade my moves with a boxer's talent until I give up, exhausted!
In public places, I'm the one they look out for, lest I get swallowed up by the world!

Some electric light points at home,
have me imitating,
a pogo stick.
I have an audience,

in my family, who seem to enjoy the free entertainment. They don't even bother to offer assistance.

The long, errr..the 'short' and short of it,
is, 'Inheritance of Short',
is what I got.

FAMILY MATTERS

First, this is suicide.
The very birth of this concept in my mind.
It is Hara-kiri.

At this point I am feeling quite brave.
Throwing caution to the winds,
am going to simply go ahead and dive headlong,
with utter disregard to personal safety!!

The only grey area in my atheist brain,
is, who decides where you get born?!
It would be rather nice to be able to choose,
be presented with an array of options.
But it's more like boom and hello!
Mom - Dad.
How do you do?
They smile and mouth their I love yous.
With time, the mollycoddling turns pretty lack lustre.
The cuteness quotient you are born with,
lasts so long as your mouth doesn't utter!!

You are also an inseparable part,
flesh, blood and genes,
of a larger specter.
The great extended Family.
They are a very good reason,
to have kinship outside the kin.

Take for instance,
whom I'd like to call the 'Gastronomic fright'.
Oh, they love food.
Food is God.
There is a tacit understanding,
that edibles, are to be revered.
(And trust me, they could write a 10-volume thesis on the various kind).
So, if they want to shower blessings and express adoration,
you are fed.

Once you cross the threshold,

you are held captive and are served an array of delicacies along with their rich and historical backgrounds.

Food is also the cure for heartbreak, work trouble, relationship issues, the moody blues et al.

There is very little that a sumptuous meal and sugar overload cannot solve.

And you cannot refuse the hospitality.

It's blasphemy (Nero would have been a willing victim).

Your bloated stomach begins bursting at the seams.

Mouth cannot chew anymore.

The very sight of the varied cuisine makes you nauseous.

You literally stagger out holding onto your stomach, which feels like you ingested a ton of bricks.

And crash out for three days.

Your friends wonder why you look ashen at the sight of *'gajar halwa'* or *'pooris'!*

Then comes the one who could make Hippocrates Corpus look bleak and incomplete.

The various ailments are medallions worn with pride.

You are enlightened with causes and symptoms

of the ghastliest of diseases. You shudder and gawk,

and wish temporary deafness.

Relentessly, the manic tirade segues,

to the description of excreted substances in various shapes, consistencies, and sizes.

You are ready to kill or die.

This one is an encyclopaedia on all the exotic, unpronounceable difficult names of curatives.

Chinese ones included and could easily outdo any pharmacy business!

Then there are these 'scanners'.

They mean well am sure.

But, crossing paths with them is like going through an x-ray machine!

Something that can look through your brain.

You are scrutinised,

head to toe, and again.

You begin to wonder if you forgot to don a vital part of a garment!!

Or suddenly developed a striking resemblance to an escaped convict!!

They also run an additional surveillance to get the inside dope on you.

Parenting tips,

those you get absolutely on the house.

You are doing it all wrong according to these expert specialists.

From an appalling diet, which could make your kid look like a Kwashiorkor victim with rickets, on the one hand,

and, suffer from all the problems associated with being obese!

You learn to nod in agreement with all the scenarios.
With a guilt-ridden expression (which pleases these certain few of course!).

You are also told very explicitly, not to expect any affection from your kids when they grow up,
as you naturally grow older.
Because you have psychologically traumatised them with too much,
or too little of everything, in that order!!
You wish you could just disappear.

How can I miss out on those,
who come to stay,
and stay and stay and stay....

And they do not even notice,
when you quietly leave your own home,
for some quiet and peace!!

When they finally snap out of their amnesiac state,
your relief is huge.
And you return to what was yours!

But,
It takes you a while,
to adjust and settle,
and you cannot find anything.
Since your home now looks like someone else's!!

At times your blood boils,
at family ties.
You want to draw blood,
and be rid.
And not belong either.
But blood is indeed thicker than water!

Near perfect, well, that would be me.
My linen, in neat stacks,
facing outward with rounded edges.
Hangers in closets,
hooks on one side.
Sheets pulled crisp and tight.
Creases, on my bed.
Oh, what a thought!!

I like my books placed,
in the alphabetical order.
You can't get away with,
displacing my cushions,
chairs or toaster!
Misaligned wall art,
really gets my goatee.
My kids,
think it's OCD.
Ha!
They just don't like it when I know exactly which one 'borrowed' my things.

OCD

I am in awe of people,
for whom, every place feels like home.
Good Lord! Not me.
I shudder and squirm,
at the mere notion,
of mass usage of space and commodities.

A visit to the physician,
is what I would, dodge and evade,
till I am almost hitching a ride with *Yama*.
So flailing and struggling, I am dragged to the house of doom.

Right from the doorknobs to the patient's seat,
it really is a disgusting bacterial feast.
How can I not cringe,
at what kind of bum,
occupied the swirling stool before mine?

The trick to opening public doors,
is what I have mastered of course.
It is all about agility and finesse.
Wait for someone else to hold the handle,
stand right behind, kind of close,
whistle perhaps or smile,
while edging in, sidling like a crab,
slinking in quick and sprite.
Yes! it's a winner.

I am also not sure if I make a good host,
or even exhibit signs of being nice to the guest(s).
It's possible, I have a nickname, something like 'Crabby Hag' or 'Grumpy Crone'.
Maybe even a 'Boo Radley' or 'Aunt Scrooge'.
I have heard folk mumble under their breath,
and break into quick smiles as I pass them by.

Well, you'd wonder, why then, would we have visitors?
Oh! that's an easy one to blame on the man of the house!

Well, for starters,
I am not a fan of shaking hands.
Never quite sure where they've been.
A hug then?
Nope,
Too much touch.

A quick buss on a cheek?
Not really, no thanks!
I'd rather a hello!
A cheery howdy do.

Besides,
I am unable to maintain,
polite conversation,
when my attention,
is focused entirely on my carpets and their (guests) shoes.

It could be a kind of dance,
every time my drawing room is invaded.
I greet people at the edge of my carpet,
we do a left, right, back and forth,
with me blocking their path,
while directing glances towards the sofas.
I even remove my footwear and claim the carpet.
It works for a bit and then it doesn't.
My pristine carpet, is a magnet.
Shouldn't people know the difference between a foot mat and a carpet!!

And then I spend a large part of the evening thinking of how to remove the stains from spills and muddy shoes.

Symmetry is so important.
Right?

So it really gets my goat,
when my cushions and curios,
are subjected to displacement.

Whilst the Man plays the perfect host,
I grumble and mumble.
Frown and scowl.
My forced smile,
must really look like a snarl!

I am also convinced,
the accompanying little people,
are not quite as naive.
Oh they're tiny imposters.
Sneaky little nosy parkers.
They peep, prod and
snoop around.
Invariably, their meddlesome ways,
play truant with my only friends.
My treasure trove of books.
Subjected heartlessly to dog ears and splotchy stains.
Strewn about and uprooted from their classified order.
Oh! what a bother!!

I do earn my pound of flesh.
When I glare at them and begin to look like the monster under their beds!!

I have to admit,
I am quite a picture of complaisance,
if I have four legged visitors.
The chaperoning humans are welcome by default.
They can always be ignored!!

Furthermore,
my furry friends,
would never accuse me,
of being afflicted,
with OCD!

• • •

XX CHROMOSOME

Unafraid.

Proud.

Determined.

Kind and Giving.

Resilient and Strong.

Unparalleled.

FEAR IS NOT THE KEY

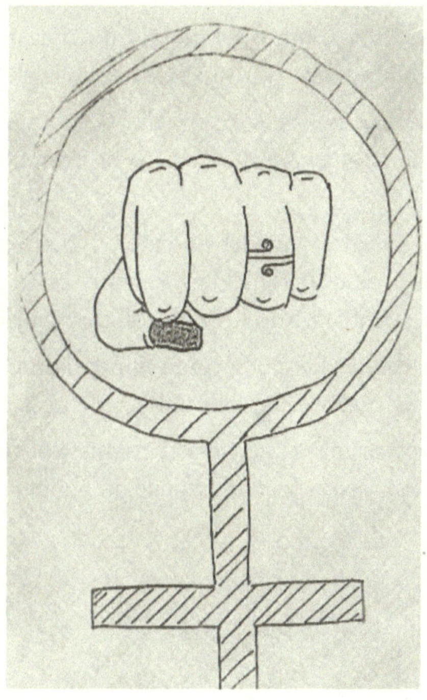

At age 13,

She: Maa, is it ok for me to go to the market in this outfit?

(She sports a deep blue sleeveless dress, going down to just above her knees).

Me: Absolutely ok.

She: I've worn cycling shorts too.

I hug her and tell her she looks fine.

Her uncertainty niggles, it's never been expressed before.

Anyhow we drive to the decided destination.

She steps out of the car; we begin to walk and I watch her closely.

She hunches over a bit, eyes mostly downcast. Infact, she determinedly does not want to meet anyone's eyes.

In the shop, she is not sure of the decency of the shop boy and is acutely aware of a bunch of teen boys hanging around.

All of this is not planned behaviour. I realize, it's in her subconscious mind. It tells her, "Beware, be as unobtrusive as possible, avoid attention brought upon yourself".

This voice teaches her to become blind and deaf to all the lewd remarks, lascivious looks and crude gestures.

She has grown up to the horrid reality of the universal objectification, disrespect and abuse of women.

Age 17,

Dressed in her 'Little Black Dress'.

Me: Kiddo, isn't this a bit short? You know how boys are at this age.

She (wide eyed)**:** I can't believe you are saying this! I am dressed for me, I am comfortable, even if I wear a full length veil, the inherent mentality won't change. I think I can pack in a few punches at the right place in case of inappropriate behaviour.

And mamma, there are decent boys around too!

I feel a little small having stereotyped 'all' boys. So, I mouth a sorry at that. She gives me her typical reassuring hug.

I look at her, poised, confident, looking uber chic and stylish. I cannot argue against her self-confidence.

I also know this bravado though applaud worthy will hold good only so much.

I need for her to be cleverer by way of defending herself against physical might.

It can't be in the way we dress or that we may like a drink too, or dance with complete abandon.

How a three-year-old or an infant, can be provocative is beyond comprehension.

We conduct ourselves, with poise, dignity and self-assuredness.

We excel at what we do.

We can multitask brilliantly, match the other gender in all spheres, perhaps outdo them in certain areas.

Yet, we are the ones that live with insecurities that have nothing to do with our capabilities.

Yet, we as guardians of our daughters will continue to advise them on dressing conservatively, or not venturing out unchaperoned after dark.

Or not drinking.

Or we ask them to don the invisibility cloak in certain situations.

We all know these are desperate attempts.

We do not caution our sons.

They have unrestricted freedom.

The streets lit and unlit, bustling market places, functioning offices, universities, hotels, even homes, day or night, will always have some power hungry, frustrated subhuman waiting to unleash his filth on an unsuspecting prey.

In war (religious or territorial or any other kind) or in peace, perpetrating acts of savagery on the female gender somehow becomes a benchmark of power.

There really is no reason other than violence.

Frustration, low self-worth or delusional male superiority are some excuses too.

The ugliest face of patriarchy, makes outraging a woman's modesty easy.

The apathy is shameful. Incidents that come to light are made much of and forgotten in the blink of an eye, until the next and the next...and the next...

Drawing a parallel to one of the most heinous crimes, we have this famous personality mouthing utter nonsense about his experience during a certain filming. Well, since the entire episode was such an ordeal for him, people who did go and watch the performance were merely being voyeuristic!

So, where does it all end?

It doesn't.

Period.

The one born with two X chromosomes has been a victim of objectification since the inception of mankind.

Nothing is going to change.

Punchline...

Do what feels right and not for the sake of anyone and certainly not because you fear you will be abused.

Dos and don'ts will and still won't protect you.

So, for a start I let my 17-year-old make a choice, not based on her attire, but because I think, fear is not the key.

THE X FACTOR

I am in perfect health.
Athletic, sporty, young.
At the threshold of life.
Of considerably sound mind.

But I feel sick.
I feel trapped like a person with a terminal illness.
Does anyone know what it is like,
to never be free of fear?
To know that no moment outside your home can be taken as is.
To always have to be guarded, alert.

Morals,
taught or imbibed, profess,
do not take what is not yours.
But my dignity is taken,
on the streets, markets....
in public and in private.

Everyone has an opinion,
on my conduct and character.
On how I should live and dress,
how I should follow a certain path,
this one lifetime on earth.

Do not steal,
but my modesty is robbed,
by ugly lascivious leers,
by rough, coarse, brusque touches,
by risqué, salacious and obscene thoughts.

And I am blamed,
for inviting trouble,
because of the way I smiled or tilted my neck.
Or I danced with too much abandon,
or I exhibited too much self-assuredness.

Do not trespass they say,
but my entire being is a thoroughfare.

Do not kill,
but I am slaughtered without mercy.
My body and soul massacred heartlessly.

Temples, churches, mosques,
abodes of the Gods,
symbols of purity and veneration.
Boundaries are duly maintained herein.
No one dares to do otherwise.
Fearing the wrath of the supreme.

Isn't the same true,
for me?
My body is MY heaven.
It houses my soul.
It houses life.
How then, is it,
so simple to defile?

Somehow,
God is everywhere.
Just that, when I need him,
He is nowhere.

THE HEART WANTS WHAT IT WANTS

Because, your gender is not a measure of what your heart desires.

At the precipice he stands,
arms splayed, widespread and winged.
It's only a tilt to eternity.
The zephyr, shaping notes across his chiselled features.
And a classical symphony unfolds.
Heightened senses rapt with pleasure.
There are no shackles to bind his mind here.

Rhythm pounds in his head.
And his heart knows the cadent beat.
A rhapsody throbs in his veins.
Bursting forth, unfettered into a powerful crescendo.

Herein, he finds his God.
This is his prayer.
His allegiance and ecstasy.
His immortality.

But,
he is the scion.
The bearer of the exalted name.
The inheritance is his albatross.

And,
he also knows,
he is the shepherd of this legacy supreme.

Aristocratic and regal.
Her proud poise, belies her agonising turmoil.
Her unflinching gaze,
patrician, intrepid and resolute,
is synonymous with her strength absolute.

She wishes to prevail.
To be the inheritor, the successor.
The carrier.

Caressing the sharp lines of the royal crest,
her nimble fingers wrap around the hilt.
The grooves and niches are deep,
they meld and yield to her grip.
With the deftness of a seasoned warrior,
she lifts the scimitar,
shredding the target to smithereens.

But,
she knows.
He is the scion.
Bearer of the exalted name.

The Patriarch knows.
He hears it in the wind.
He senses it in his old bones,
in the rustle of the susurrant leaves,
in the dead of the silent nights,
in the eyes of the multitude.
Hopeful, anguished.
He knows,
a harbinger of doom,
hangs, poised,
over his precious land.

The Royal Sceptre,
the symbol of allegiance and honour,
the keeper of the land's pride and glory,
the beholder of a new beginning,
the delegator of trust and duty,
awaits.
Awaits a deserving successor.

In the glow of a thousand lamps,
a confluence stands.
Expectant of a verdict.
Of a decree to come forth.
Their land had a legacy to bequeath.

The majestic ancestor rises.
Still stately and grand in his stature.
Wisdom etched across his features.
He holds forth,
the royal symbol of adjudication,
and as a final obeisance to the land,
hands the sceptre,
to his daughter.

ESSE

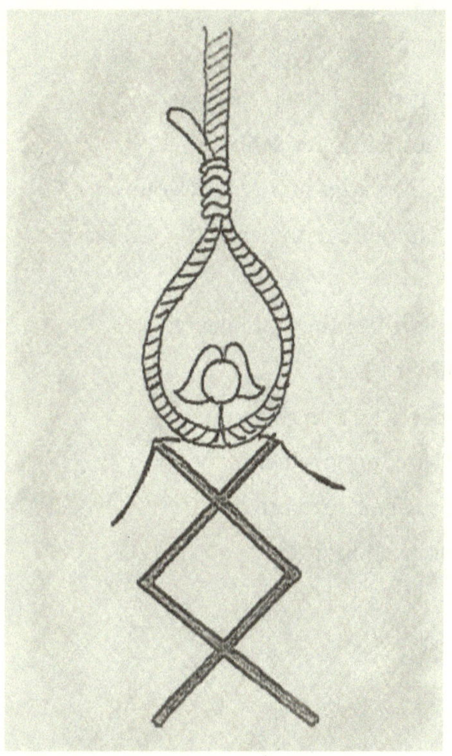

The weight of her love,
broke her.
Her belly sagging with the burden,
bearing down, heavy, stubborn and demanding.

The heavy torrential rain,
calmed her fragile nerves.
She could weep with abandon.
Scream her pain away.

The sharp stinging drops were her ally.
The cold, numbing her aching.
The water, like balm on her sore soul.
A perfect camouflage to her unhinged tears.

She could still feel the little heart,
in rhythm with hers,
her little parts forming from hers,
her blood flowing into her,
her love coursing through her,
her soul nourishing hers.

She knew every nuance,
the almond eyes,
rose bud lips,
the little button nose,
the little fingers she had imagined would be entwined with hers.

She had seen the sun aglow,
in her auburn curls.

She had heard her whisper,
an endearment, a name,
her bosom swelling with love.
She had heard her gurgling laughter.
She had seen her moue.
She had tasted her.
Smelt her.
Breathed her.

She had tried,
but,
the executioners,
did not know any of this.

For them,
The privilege life,
belonged to a certain set of chromosomes.

This, she did not know.

•••

THE X Y Z GENERATION

Hopefully only the end of the alphabetic order and not civilization.

WHAT CHILDREN WANT

Children (aged 10 onwards), have the entire older generation as confused as tangled threads of wool.

This is the era that has seen the maximum number of parenting guides, via media of all kinds, social, visual, auditory, etcetera and not leaving the older generation any wiser but foxed as never before.

Dos and don'ts, hows and whys. A multitude of psychological bantering that makes you feel you did the most awful job at parenting.

A terrible burden. What if you turned your kid into a psychotic killer or a wimp. A selfish egotist or a loser?

You analyse and introspect, assess your psychological wellbeing and parenting skills. You are just about ready to do anything to make life as perfect as possible for your child. You truly want to be a good parent.

You do everything, except follow your instinct, which at times tells you to just maroon the kids on an island for a week at the least.

Your attempts are desperate, especially because your life is like 'The Truman Show'. Your angry spluttering face may be plastered all over Snap Chat with a caption "Mom or Monster!". It could be a selfie of your child against an 'aesthetically depressing' backdrop. A dimly lit room or a patchy wall with unmentionable graffiti posted on Instagram, with a quote, "Isn't it sad when you get hurt so much, you can finally say, I am used to it".

You are obviously going to freak out and are on the verge of getting professional help and curse yourself for whatever you did to hurt the kid this bad.

You are just about to fix an appointment with the 'best' counsellor when your Facebook notification shows the same 'on the brink kid' doing the hoopla with a friend!

You are completely at sea!!

You, as a mom and dad, will be put on the stand, judged and declared guilty. Of course, you will be redeemed, just be patient and wait to be grandparents! That will be the sweetest ever taste of victory.

For children today,

More is never enough.

Enough is less.

And less is nothing!!

The harder you try,

the greater the trial.

We are like the Genie who is just tired of "Your wish is my command". We need to arm ourselves against ourselves.

Perhaps we need to amend the greatest poser of all times. Perhaps the focus should shift now.

Women have been in the limelight for far too long, ever since the creation of the first pair. Eve, the poor cursed one, took the blame. Adam simply bobbed his apple, awe struck by Eve.

The rest is history.

No one told Pandora not to open the box. She was only, literally clay moulded into a woman by the Greek Gods.

Isn't it getting kind of stodgy, like a repetitive broken record about women being a mystery, unpredictable? Agreed we women are a fantastic potpourri. Sometimes an enigma.

But this age belongs to our children. So, the question of the century should be:

What Children Want.

DEAR KNOW-IT-ALL

Just stop awhile.
Slow down.
Quit rushing, running.
Give your life a calm thought.
It will help you move in the right direction,
instead of going off on a wild goose chase.

Breathe.
Savour the good things in life.
Take deep breaths.
Inhale and exhale and again.
So you do not gasp and splutter for a mere breath.

Luxuriate and relish flavours, allow them to roll off of your tongue.
Savour what goes into your mouths,
instead of merely wolfing down edibles,
not knowing sweet from sour or salty from tangy.

Pause at times,
to listen to the birds.
It's the sweetest sound ever.
Sweeter than your mum yelling,
A rather pleasant start to the day.

Listen to the sound of silence.
Oh yes! believe me that is when,
you'll really listen, listen to your soul,
To your overwrought brain.

Admire the sunset,
the sunrise.
Try it sometime,
so, you can brag to the future generations,
about something called the SUN.

Feel the breeze blow gently across your features.
Inhale the scent of the flowers.
Yes, flowers exude perfumes quite different from the ones sprayed by your partners.

Dress well.
Get decent haircuts.
You might like to show your kids some of your pictures.

Raise your bent heads from those screens.
Perhaps you might interact with your kin while you still recognise them.

It might also save you,
from ending up looking like hunchbacked extra-terrestrials.
Above all, stop and look at your folks.

Dad's dad.

He's okay if you never bathe or eat off the floor.

You want food and clean clothes you have to revere mom.

Like, really esteem her.

Grovelling helps a lot!!

Look at the lines of labour etched across her body.

Like bloody hell.

ALL OVER!

And mind you the scars are not limited only physically.

Having your stomach stretched as if it were a balloon with super elasticity (wonder if science has invented such an elastic).

Your precious anatomy warped out of shape never to be the same again.

You darned well be grateful!

Spare some time for family.

Well, time is money!!

On a good day, you could get rich!

Finally, you're lucky to be where you are.

Can you imagine yourselves as parents and us as your kids?!!

Just the thought sets my mind working like a tornado.

I'd REALLY like that though.

• • •

THE FLAUTIST

You descended into a tumultuous world, keeping the order. Well, the balance is tipping again.

ODE TO KRISHNA

Wrecked, ravaged and brutalised.
Barren, joyless, parched and suppressed.
Such was the turmoil in *Mathura's* land.
Tormented under *Kansa's* rule of tyranny.
Blasphemous and barbaric, he was evil's progeny.
Inebriated with his invincible stature,
his gluttony surpassed all boundaries of nature.

Mathura's gloom,
Steadily grew each day,
under a cloud of dismal doom.

Gods in heaven, cursed this Satan.
Distressed and furious at this diabolical situation,
plotted to slay this arrogant demon.
A warning was in order.

All of *Aryavrata* heard the voice thunder.
"Cruelty and terror would no longer reign,
earth would be blessed with His presence benign".

Obsessed and terrified of the divine prophecy,
of his destruction at the hands of an infant,

Kansa had *Mathura* at his mercy.
Nary a house was spared his wrath.
Heartlessly slayed each life on earth.
Terrified parents, begged and pleaded,
cajoled and bribed,
offered their own lives instead.
But the monster was unstoppable.
His cruelty unimaginable.

Stately trees grew old and wan.
Scarred, helpless, shattered and broken,
standing witness to this outrageous massacre.
With not a soul to match the ogre.

Birds would no longer tweet or sing,
fearing what horror each day would bring.
The forests were bereft of sound.
Only the darkness of death was all around.
Childless homes devoid of laughter.

The worm-infested creature,
wouldn't even spare his sister.
Ordained prison and chains for *Vasudev* and *Devaki*.
Advice for decorum, incited a fit inconceivable.
Inhuman, vicious and vile,
barked orders unfit for even the worst criminal.

The cursed couple, in shackles lay,
manacled all night and day.
The conception was miraculous.
Surpassing all realms of earthly hindrances.

As *Devaki's* womb flowered,
and her belly swelled,
she felt a yearning, a gratitude, deep and profound.
Pure ecstasy filled her being.
Oh! how she longed, how her heart ached,
to envelop in her arms this inseparable part.
This part of her soul and being.
To hold to her bosom and to protect forever,
her child, her God.
The saviour of the world.

When God decided,
to don the garb of a human child,
a quiet stillness befell all around.
A silence so serene,
not a leaf stirred or rustled.
The air stopped it's breathing.
Time became a slave.
Life took a little pause.
It was the only allegiance to the supreme.
Each soul for that instant, became one with the universe.
In unison, they achieved Nirvana.
Each being feeling blessed.
Sleep was only a medium.

Devaki was rapturous.
Her soul at peace.
As if in reverence and awe,
the shackles too, lay limp and futile.

Satiated, slaked and quenched,
the *Yamuna* swelled.
Twisted and turned,
lurched and lunged.
Voluptuous and serpentine slithered across and beyond.
With pride,
gurgled like a child.
Flaunting her supremacy unabashedly.
Between *Indra* and her,
it was a magnificent medley.
He roared and thundered.
She danced to the copious showers.
It was a glorious celebration of powers.
For therein lay the knowledge, the wisdom,
of promises unspoken,
of a birth, extraordinary,
of a form, pure and Godly.

KANHA

His skin, dark as the night.
His name synonymous with it.
A seraphic aura enveloping him.

Curls that run like rivulets,
unruly and untamed.
A rich plume of blue adorning his hair,
a single feather with an eye surrounded by an explosion of blue.
Rose bud lips concealing a mischievous smile,
that light up his eyes.
Little pendulums dancing in his ear lobes.
Clad in only a *dhoti.*
A bare torso embellished with garlands of marigold.
Little Krishna, beloved and cherished,
holds within him the absolute power of love.

Held captive and poisoned by the serpent *Kalia*,
the *Yamuna*, infested with the toxic venom,
turned black and ran riot.
As many lay dying, having drunk from the lethal waters,
Krishna but a mere child faced the mighty snake.
A terrible duel followed hence.

The enormous creature wrapped little *Krishna* in a deathly embrace,

knowing he'd squeeze the life out of the boy.

The monster watched befuddled as the child

slithered out deftly,

and stood atop his fanned head and performed the cosmic dance, his tiny feet carrying the weight of the entire universe.

As the humungous creature crumpled into a mangled heap, the *Yamuna* changed colour.

Rid of the evil, she flowed, clear as crystal, sparkling with utter joy.

Swallowed, once by a giant demon bird *Krishna* emerges unharmed.

Inside the *asura,* he generates intense heat,

forcing the monster to open his beak thus releasing the young lad.

Krishna then pries his beak apart killing the feared *Bakasura.*

Indra, the lord of heaven,

sat smug with his unparalleled status, of being the undisputed lord.

When whispers of a rival, divine and loved threatened his stature, he raged with envy.

He lashed out with torrential rain,

pouring ceaselessly, unrelenting, sharp as knives.

He hurtled bolts of lightning and thundered expletives.

Kanha, the lad, hefted the indomitable *Govardhan.*

It stood perched atop his little finger light as a feather.

Protected from the vicious deluge that lasted a week, the people and animals alike knew they were in extraordinary company.

The taste of the earth slaked His hunger pangs.

Eyes twinkling mischievously, He'd fill his mouth with mud.

Denied the deed when confronted by *Yashodha.*

Exasperated with his antics she asked him to open his mouth,

Just like an ordinary child, he obeyed.

Swirling within was the entire universe.

As she enveloped baby *Krishna* into an embrace

Yashoda's eyes brimmed,

with love,

with gratitude,

with reverence,

with peace,

with absolute surrender.

Perhaps, the charm of little *Kanha* lay in his complete naiveté that he was divine.

THE FAVOURITE

Sprinkling silver, the luminous orb, sat smug amidst the diamond studded sky.

The earth rapturous, intoxicated with the scent of Jasmine.

The breeze carrying dreams and whispering sweet nothings.

It was a night of a million promises.

The universe glowed with love.

Each movement precise, she adorned herself slowly.

Heavily kohled eyes possessively ensconced His image.

Her lips red with betel trembled as she uttered His name.

Her tresses ran like rivulets along her back, embellished with pearls of *mogra*, diffusing a heady aroma.

Her face luminous with tenderness, she waited.

Her being sensitive, alert, to each sound.

When the flute filled her senses, she unfolded like a bud unfurling, yearning, yielding.

As her eyes, moist with love, settled on Him,

the confusing overlap of emotions was split second as he enveloped her in his arms.

Wringing herself free, she stared with disbelief, indignation, anger.

His body was swathed with the fragrance of roses, like an attar.

His eyes tired, red and droopy.

He looked dishevelled, drained.

An aura of languor enveloping Him.

His torso stretched lazily, marked with traces of having loved another with complete abandon.

Nail marks on his broad chest were reminiscent of fiery passion.

Blotches of Kohl on His lips having brushed against another's eyes, ran in uneven lines.

Her heart broke into a million pieces as she surveyed Him, her senses acute to every nuance of His vulnerability.

He enfolded her in a tight embrace.

His eyes twinkling with mischievous love,

attempting to placate her with the assurance of His eternal love.

He reasons with her of having been bruised by thorns while He had plucked flowers for her.

He had been seeking the sweetest fruit for her hence the delay.

Affirming His love, He denied ever having been with another.

He, the Flautist, *Madhava*, with the sweetness of honey, creates magic as his fingers dance.

The flute pays obeisance to him and melds to his touch.

The melodies cast a spell all around.

The universe in a trance, sits still, calm and satiated.

His love transcends all that is tellurian.

Yet, even He is drawn, almost like an addict to her.

To her love, pure and limitless, generous, determined, relentless, selfless, steadfast.

It becomes etched in His heart.

She completes Him like no other.

She pines for His love, earthly and raw.
To be one with Him.
To be His only one.

The knowledge that He is air.
He is water.
He is the earth.
He is the sky and beyond,
does not alleviate her pain.
Her love will, for eternity, remain unrequited.

*Inspired by an Ashtapadi from Jayadev's Gita Govind.

ACKNOWLEDGEMENTS

The frailty of humans lies in the desire to be loved and to be heard.

If slaked, there is nothing more fulfilling.

Eternally grateful to those who have loved me so and for the blessings that they are. You all know who you are.

ADDENDUM

Naturally, this book could not have been possible without me.

Illustrations for some of the pieces have been done by my mother, fondly known as 'Nani'. Through the process I did act difficult, quite like a rebellious teen. I'd like to thank her like an adult. Also, for her unwavering support and encouragement. Most parents like to entrap unsuspecting guests by asking their kid(s) to perform. All the while hearts swelling with pride at the recitation of 'Jack and Jill'. Well! I did surpass the recitation level! So, I let her toot without resistance.

A special mention to my daughter who is the keeper of memories in our home. She has managed to capture many beautiful moments I had with Nuts.

A big Thank You for keeping the love alive.

www.ingramcontent.com/pod-product-compliance
Lightning Source LLC
LaVergne TN
LVHW041204150826
845673LV00001B/278